# Exterior
# DETAILS

# Exterior
# DETAILS

An inspirational and practical guide
to transforming the *outside* of your home

### by
## JOCASTA INNES

Foreword by
Melanie Fleischmann

Leslie Garisto
Consulting Editor

with contributors

**Susan Conder**
Exterior Diversity

**Penny David**
Focus on Detail

**Yvonne Rees**
The Larger View

**Susan Conder and Leslie Garisto**
Directory

Simon and Schuster

New York   London   Toronto   Sydney   Tokyo   Singapore

SIMON AND SCHUSTER
Simon & Schuster Building
Rockefeller Center
1230 Avenue of the Americas
New York, New York, 10020

SIMON AND SCHUSTER and colophon are registered trademarks of
Simon & Schuster Inc.

Conceived and produced by
Anness Law Limited
4a The Old Forge
7 Caledonian Road
London N1 9DX

Editorial direction: Lewis Esson Publishing, London

Art direction: Adrian Morris

Text editors: Sarah Chapman, Leslie Garisto

Picture research: Jennie Karrach

First published in Great Britain in 1990 by Collins and Brown Limited.

Typeset in Great Britain by Central Southern Typesetters, Eastbourne

Printed and bound in Hong Kong

1  3  5  7  9  10  8  6  4  2

Library of Congress Cataloging in Publication Data

Exterior details: an inspirational and practical guide to
    transforming the outside of your home/[compiled] by Jocasta Innes
    ; foreword by Melanie Fleischmann ; Leslie Garisto, consulting
    editor.
        p.        cm.
    "First published in Great Britain in 1990 by Collins and Brown
Limited"—T.p. verso.
    ISBN 0-671-72576-9
    1.  Building—Details.  2.  Exterior walls.  3.  Garden structures.
I. Innes, Jocasta.
TH2025.E97      1991
698—dc20                                          90—36221
                                                      CIP

Page one: A weathervane on stables in Connecticut.
Frontispiece: Door of a converted windmill in
West Chiltington, West Sussex.
Opposite: Fanlight in Stonington, Connecticut.

# CONTENTS

# FOREWORD

It is a great honor to be asked to write the foreword to any book, but this one is especially close to my heart – I happen to be a great Jocasta Innes fan! When I heard that the woman whose books had enlivened the inside of our house had adjusted her sights to exteriors, my first, and selfish, thought was 'now, why didn't I think of that?'.

The answer, of course, is that it's just as well that I didn't. Jocasta Innes is the person for the job. Who else can take centuries of history, design, techniques and any number of other bits of information, and come out with a book that isn't intimidating, but is downright encouraging?

*Exterior Details* is the quintessential ideas book. Here you have that file you always kept, stuffed with clips of things you liked and might add to your house some day. There are beautiful photographs of porches and overdoors, pathways and plantings. But the file has been organized. So now when you want that idea about an awning that you liked so much, you can find it easily here. Not only that, but the file has been embellished. You also get historical information, which I find fascinating, and you get advice (from an expert) about appropriateness.

By that, I don't mean to imply that the book gives you lists of do's and, more stultifying, don'ts. Rather the opposite. For example, if I thought about concrete at all, I thought of it as something appropriate to twentieth-century architecture. I would have assumed that for any historic structure, it was taboo. Little did I know, until I read this text, that it was used by the Romans, sometimes faced(!) with stone, brick, or terracotta. Well, I have a few friends who love to turn up their noses when they hear about facing anything, and think only an uneducated low-life would contemplate putting concrete anywhere. I can't wait to tell them.

*Exterior Details* is full of treats like that. As you'd expect, it also reveals a few trade secrets — things like how to get that perfect, enviable, high-gloss finish on your door. So, fellow idea-hoarders, chuck those files. And, one more time, thank you, Jocasta Innes.

MELANIE FLEISCHMANN

# INTRODUCTION

The first surprise – and a pleasing one – that this book has in store for its readers is the discovery that houses too have faces, or façades, and that house faces are as exuberantly diverse in every particular – colour, shape, proportion, detail – as human faces. Reassuringly, in a world where working environments increasingly wear a look of rubber-stamped conformity, private home environments remain an area where individualism is not only alive and well, but flourishing – thanks to the example of the media and the spread of DIY as never before.

It must be abundantly clear to anyone leafing through *Exterior Details,* that people the world over care a lot about the way their homes look outside, and that they put much thought, effort and imagination into projecting an attractive image to the passing world. Because, of course – and it is a slightly sobering thought – what one does to the exterior of one's home – in most contexts, urban or rural – affects a lot of other people: not simply visitors, friends, or neighbours, but the passing world. It is a little like having a picture on permanent exhibition. It is a challenge and a responsibility.

Making something beautiful happen outside one's home – whether it is painting the whole thing an uplifting colour like saffron yellow or Wedgwood blue; or training a wisteria to droop shaggy mauve clusters up the ironwork; or clipping a fat topiary hen or chessman out of the front hedge – is as nice an example of

enlightened self interest as you could hope to find. It makes a good impression on strangers, but it also contributes its mite to the sum of human happiness. Have you ever noticed how often exteriors and their detail figure in the art and literature of the world?

Another surprise to emerge from the gallery of building types – primitive and hi-tech, vernacular and grand, lushly rural and trimly urban – is that, through all the surface diversity, certain lineaments persist in different places, different times. Spotting a family likeness between a lattice verandahed house in the West Indies and a stuccoed terrace in Brighton is not only fun, but a painless grounding in the history of architecture. It makes you question the enduring popularity of particular styles of building, of porch structures, glazing bars, even window-boxes. There is a steadily growing interest in authenticity, the real thing, appropriateness in all areas of life today. Architecturally, this is expressed in a growing respect for traditional and historical precedent – in a word, enlightened conservation!

No one should feel shackled by the past, but on the other hand, it does not hurt to be reminded that one's house is part of a wider scheme of things: architectural, social and historical. Vividly, entertainingly, this is what the text and photographs in this book spell out, whether you are reading it in Tuscany, Taiwan, or some other corner of our global village.

JOCASTA INNES

*Green paintwork on a cottage
in Romania's Transylvanian
forests.*

# EXTERIOR DIVERSITY

Until the growing uniformity of the Modern Age, homes
varied widely in different parts of the world.
Local considerations, such as climate, materials and building
practices, produced very distinctive regional looks; and
ornament was usually the signature of local craftsmen. Even
architectural fashions were liberally adapted to embrace local
styles. A survey of this rich diversity sets the scene.

*Left: The grand 'painted
ladies' of Old San Francisco,
contrasted with the modern
skyline of its financial centre.
Above: Rooftops in
Dubrovnik, Yugoslavia.*

The word 'façade' from the Latin *facies*, for face, has come to mean the main face, or elevation, of a building, as seen from the street or public space. It can also mean, more generally, the mask-like outward appearance of a thing, as distinct from its inner character. The earliest and most primitive house façades presented a simple, unpretentious face to the outside world: survival, rather than prettiness, was the highest priority. As civilization advanced and societies became more stable, house façades began to be built to be admired, and to convey information about the wealth, occupation or rank in the community of those who lived behind them, and perhaps also their military power, taste or their commitment to the current fashion.

Today, house façades continue to transmit this information, but with a visual language that can transcend geographical, cultural and historical boundaries. While most house interiors consist simply of a series of interconnected cubic spaces, the style of their façades varies enormously. Originally designed according to such factors as prevailing geography, period of construction and architectural fashion, they have often become disconnected from their roots. The unique character of individual localities, with buildings derived from local materials and culture, has often been diluted or destroyed by the use of cheaper, transported materials and the spread of a common culture by the mass media.

In many countries, planning regulations and laws help protect the integrity of local domestic style, or 'vernacular' (from the Latin for home-born slave), by preserving existing buildings and controlling the design of new ones. The many recently formed historical and local societies are another manifestation of our growing awareness of our heritage and our wish to preserve vernacular and more sophisticated architectural styles such as Georgian, Regency and Victorian.

## EXTERIOR STYLES

The architecture of any one country at any one time reflects a complex mixture of geographical, geological, climatic, historical, political, social, economic, technological and even religious factors. The proportions of this 'recipe' may vary. In the twentieth century, geological and religious factors play a less important role than previously, whereas 150 years ago (before new transport systems took full effect), the local geological strata played a major part in the appearance of buildings so that, for example, clay brick would be the vernacular building material for one English village and chalk or sandstone might predominate in another, a short distance away.

Certain influences may recede and then reappear in slightly different guises. The need for high security in many large cities today, for example, has resulted in the re-emergence of a defensive architecture with features of the medieval fortress: small, barred windows, single, easily controllable entrances and high, strong walls.

Climatic factors can make geographically distant houses appear uncannily similar. Hot, dry climates, for example, tend to result in the building of flat-roofed dwellings with thick, heat-reflective pale or white walls with small apertures for coolness.

Military conquests and migrations have long influenced the architecture of the host country (willing or otherwise). Roman building techniques spread throughout the Empire; immigrant Flemish craftsmen influenced English Elizabethan and Jacobean house style; and waves of English, Dutch, French, German, Spanish and Scandinavian emigrants have left an imprint on American domestic architecture, and on European colonies throughout the world. When armies return home the influence is reversed, the mother country often benefiting architecturally from imported ideas.

Modern technology is perhaps the greatest source of homogeneity, both in the technological development of ideas and in transmitting them world-wide. The nineteenth-century American invention of the elevator, for example, originally used in commercial and office buildings, allowed apartments everywhere to soar far above the usual six-storey maximum height of previous multiple-storey dwellings, while the television, which became available less than fifty years ago, transmits instant images of aspirational lifestyles, and the houses that go with them, to living rooms all over the world.

The role of housing in the development of architectural styles is a dual one. Houses for the rich, the powerful, the noble and the well educated have often been the forerunners of new styles, while ordinary housing has more modestly and quietly fed those developments countrywide.

## RAW MATERIALS

The structural materials used to build house walls can remain exposed or be hidden by a thin waterproof veneer, such as cement rendering, or by a completely different, architectural 'wallpaper' applied over an earlier, no longer fashionable, style or material. While fake stone and fake 'Tudor' beams may be frowned on today, many a Tudor or Elizabethan farmhouse was given a Georgian, Regency or Gothic facelift on its front elevation, which is now much admired, or even listed as a protected building.

Until the advent of the Industrial Revolution at the end of the eighteenth century, and the development of the great railway systems in the early nineteenth century, local raw materials were the only option for the vast majority of house builders. Local brickyards, quarries and forests provided the goods, and local artisans and craftsmen brought their own traditions and techniques of construction to bear. The result was a visual coherence between the buildings of a particular village, hamlet or city. There was also a visual compatibility between the buildings and the landscape, since the raw materials mirrored local geology and flora, and responded to the local weather conditions.

### Mud

Mud – wet soil with a high clay, or clay and lime, content – is one of the oldest and commonest raw materials for building, used either as solid material on its own or as infill between timber frames. Mud has no tensile strength, so mass mud walls are thick, held in

*New and old exterior styles stand side by side in Cologne, Germany.*

*Above: Mud can produce grandeur, as demonstrated by this building in Algeria.*

*Far left: Adobe houses of the Pueblo Indians in New Mexico. Made from mud 'bricks', smoothed together with more mud and left to dry in the sun, they make the most of abundant local natural resources.*

*Left: Mud huts in Cameroon, with simple whitewash decoration.*

place by their own weight. Building with mud is time-consuming but requires little skill, and the softly rounded edges and organic forms that mud buildings often take are pleasing to the eye.

Mud can be used in other ways, depending on its composition and the type of structure. Turf clods, mixed with straw and gravel, are used to form cob, or made into bricks which are dried in the sun before use. Mud-brick walls can be thinner than mass mud, but are only suitable in dry climates: the early Romans and ancient Egyptians built their rectangular huts of unfired mud bats; and American Pueblo Indians build their terraces of cube-shaped buildings from sun-dried mud brick. In wet climates, waterproof foundations and renderings and pitched roofs with deep overhangs protect mud walls from rain. In dry climates damp-proofing is unnecessary, and flat roofs are a practical option.

Mud is a good insulator, cool in hot climates and

warm in cool ones. Thatch is a similarly good insulator and universally available, so thatched-roofed mud houses are a feature of landscapes as diverse as Scandinavia and Africa. Today, mud as a building material has largely been superseded in the West, but Third World countries continue to use it. The outstanding Egyptian architect Hassan Fathy (1900–89) was a great proponent of mud as a building material. Much impressed by Nubian mud-brick architecture, Fathy felt that a return to this tradition was a moral and practical solution to the shortage of mass housing.

Unfired mud cannot be formed into intricate shapes, though its surface texture can vary; for example, broad bas relief is a feature of Nigerian Hausa mud homes. The patterns of the protruding wooden joists in Pueblo mud-brick dwellings form pleasant repetitive designs. Colour, whether as broad washes or in complex decorations, is an important way of embellishing mud houses.

## Timber

Wood has been used in house-building since earliest times among primitive peoples living in forested areas. It became a staple traditional building material in Britain and America and, today, with cultivated timber crops and modern transport, wood-frame houses are virtually everywhere.

Wood itself varies enormously in quality and its suitability for external use. European oak, for example, is stable, weatherproof and lasts indefinitely, and from the sixteenth century was the chosen wood for house building in England, until supplies ran out in the eighteenth century. (Before that, the cost of felling and planing oak made it beyond the means of all but the rich and the Church.) The much loved Tudor and Elizabethan black-and-white houses that survive are largely of oak, although chestnut, hornbeam and elm were also used, but these timbers, being less weatherproof, have seldom survived.

Today, commercially grown softwoods, largely conifers, provide most of the timber used for housebuilding. Unlike timber from the virgin forests, from which the denser heartwood alone was used, present available stocks are more sappy and therefore more vulnerable to rot, and must be treated with preservative if they are going to be exposed to weather or damp. The fact that most of the buildings in London in 1666 were of wood was a major factor in the Great Fire, and timber-frame houses today are often clad in fireproof slates, tiles, bricks or rendering.

Primitive wooden houses were made of wattle and daub. Branches or twigs would be built up like a tent round a central tree trunk and covered with mud; or built as a straight-sided cylindrical wall with a conical roof; or a trench would be roofed over with wattle and daub. (Charcoal burners in England were still using such dwellings less than a century ago.) Another primitive form of wooden dwelling, still used by Australian aborigines today, is the barrel-vaulted hut: both ends of a series of branches are buried in the ground to form a row of parallel arches which is then covered with smaller twigs and branches.

A more sophisticated early wooden dwelling was the log hut, as made in Sweden, Norway, Russia and the Alps, and by the early settlers in America. Solid trunks were aligned vertically or horizontally and close together, and the gaps between them packed with mud, moss or rags.

With better tools and increasing skills, planks of timber could be split or sawn and more complex timber-frame structures erected. Early ones resembled inverted ships – medieval shipbuilders were also house-builders – and typical examples were English cruck houses which had sloping walls and curving members, or crucks, with one end buried in the ground and the other meeting a keel-like wooden ridge piece. Cruck houses are the forerunners of the A-framed house, currently popular in Scandinavian countries and parts of America.

Square-framed houses have their origins in log huts, and are the most widespread form of timber house construction today. They were originally made of vertical posts, either spaced close together or widely apart, according to the availability of the wood.

The spaces were filled with lathes covered with cob and lime-washed, or, in the case of wide spacing, with woven twig panels covered with clay; these were often later replaced with brick.

Wood cladding, or weatherboarding, dates from the eighteenth century, when natural-grown oaks and similar hardwoods were replaced with less weatherproof substitutes. Traditionally built as horizontal overlapping planks, cladding is now also used vertically, Scandinavian-style, and diagonally. In America, western red cedar shingles, weathering to an attractive silvery grey untreated, or remaining an attractive reddish-brown if treated, are popular.

Wood has also long been used ornamentally. Medieval European domestic architecture is rich in carved work on beams, barge-boards and door and window frames. Non-structural carved wood decorations, usually in geometric patterns such as Elizabethan 'magpie' black-and-white, were also popular. The 'exposed' timber of mock Tudor or Elizabethan house, pub and restaurant façades is a decorative derivative of early timber cruck and frame houses. The Victorian craze for decorative sawn woodwork, thanks to the newly invented machine fretsaw, or jigsaw, produced charming exterior detail. Today, wood's natural, sympathetic surface is viewed as ornamental in its own right, compared with artificial materials such as concrete and plastics.

*Left: An early Tudor example of the English cruck house.*

*Below left: A modern A-framed house.*

*Above: Typical North-American log cabin construction.*

*Right above: Beach houses, such as the Sayer House in San Diego, California, are often still primarily of timber construction and this allows their owners and architects to make good use of wood's flexibility and to make more unorthodox statements.*

*Near right: A log chalet in Switzerland's model folk village of Ballenberg.*

*Middle right top: A classic American weatherboard house in East Haven, Connecticut. Dating from 1888, it shows typical Victorian decoration.*

*Middle right bottom: An eighteenth-century 'pioneer' house in Waitangi, New Zealand betrays some of the elements of the simple Georgian elegance then in vogue back in Britain.*

*Far right top: Another nineteenth-century American timber house in Pawtucket, Rhode Island.*

*Far right bottom: A house in Raumu, Finland.*

*Kylemore Abbey in Connemara, Eire, is built of pale stone with darker blue-grey quoins and crenellations to haunting effect. Built as a mock 'castle' by an eighteenth-century millionaire, it has been a Benedictine Abbey since 1920.*

## Stone

Stone is relatively heavy and, except for the most primitive structures, requires more skill to work than timber, brick or mud. It is fire-resistant and varies, according to type, from being fairly porous to being virtually impermeable. There are three basic types of stone. Igneous rock, such as granite and basalt, has been formed by cooling magma, and is long lasting and durable. Sedimentary rock, such as limestones, sandstones and chalk, has been built up on the sea bed and consolidated under pressure. It is made of organic remains or crumbled igneous rock. Metamorphic rock is either sedimentary or igneous rock transformed by pressure, heat, or both; marble is metamorphized limestone, and slate is also metamorphic.

Stone is one of the oldest building materials, and was used, before the days of easy transport, for all-stone houses in treeless areas, and as infill for timber frames in forested areas. Early stone huts were made from fieldstone gathered from the soil surface, which cleared the land for farming at the same time. Round stone huts were similar to early timber huts, with a beehive shape capable of withstanding strong winds at high altitudes; they occurred all over the world. Rectangular stone huts required more skill to construct the corners and roofs, but are also an ancient form, especially where animals and people shared shelter.

The Egyptians, Greeks and Romans were among the first to quarry stone. They also learned how to cut stone into regular-shaped blocks, and knew how to polish it. They used massive blocks in religious buildings, and the Romans and Greeks also used their masonry skills for houses. Their skills died with them, however, and most early medieval stone buildings were of local, natural boulders, cobbles, flints or soft sandstones.

Gothic architecture derived, in part, from the difficulty of quarrying and carrying stone, and used the available small stones in the most economical way. New quarrying skills emerged in the late Middle Ages, and fortified castles were then built of larger blocks of stone.

Throughout history, the building stone of dying or dead civilizations has provided a convenient raw material for following periods. This pilfering of history was often a by-product of military conquest, but even today, components or ornaments of stone and other materials and even slate tiles are sensibly taken from demolition sites by architectural salvage firms.

In Britain, stone's use in ordinary housing grew as timber supplies shrank. Pragmatic but attractive solutions included rubble walling with dressed stone quoins, and soft chalk or sandstone walls with harder

stone or brick quoins. Flint – irregularly shaped silica stones found in chalk – was widely used in Tudor houses, often in elaborate decorative patterns. The early American settlers used fieldstone for houses, and continued to do so for the next two centuries, especially in Pennsylvania and the Hudson River Valley.

Dressed stone was an inherent part of Palladian architecture, not only in Renaissance Europe but also as interpreted by the British during the eighteenth century and, later, in their Empire and in America. Inigo Jones and Christopher Wren used Portland stone; Classical mansions sported dressed stone quoins, door and window surrounds, and moulded cornices and balustrades. Greek and Gothic Revival styles on both sides of the Atlantic relied heavily on stone. In Australia the abundance of convict labour to work in stone resulted in impressive colonial homes.

The decorative quality of stonework comes from its shape, colour and texture and the pattern in which it is laid. Stone, which may be kept in its natural rough state or dressed to a chosen finish, varies in colour according to its composition and any impurities, such as iron, within it. Juxtaposing contrasting stones for decorative effect is an ancient art, brought to fruition in Renaissance Venice and to its extreme in the high Victorian period. Dressed stone can have various surface finishes: smooth, rusticated, hammer-dressed or

furrowed, for example. Courses can be random or squared up, with or without bonding courses. The choice and finish of mortar can enormously affect the finished appearance, and in sophisticated Classical work, joints are worked so finely that the mortar scarcely shows.

Until the advent of modern road and rail systems, local stone gave an identity to whole towns or regions: the warm yellow of Bath stone, the dour grey granite of Edinburgh, and the slate roofs of Wales were all dependent on local materials. (Exceptions included stone moved by river or sea, such as the Caen stone from Normandy used in London buildings.) The character of a stone also affected its potential for ornamental use: hard stones led to severe, plain styles, while softer stones invited carved sculpture and rich embellishment.

It is only recently that stone has become a luxury, with the cost of quarrying, transport and skilled masons pricing it out of most housing budgets. It is more affordable when used as thin slabs over cheaper walling; as flint facing for a cheaper backing; or as 'reconstructed stone', a sophisticated form of concrete made of crushed aggregate mimicking the original. Stone details such as chimney stacks, sills, copings, pavings and doorsteps are still possible, although concrete has all but superseded stone.

*Top left: Lacock Village in Wiltshire, is generally considered to be one of the most beautiful villages in England. It has many fine stone houses dating from the fifteenth to nineteenth centuries.*

*Top right: This deceptive little stone cottage, with thatched roof and vegetable garden, is actually part of the fantasy in the grounds of Versailles' Petit Trianon.*

*Above left: Stone houses in the village of Eze between Cannes and Nice in the south of France.*

*Above: The character and versatility of stone exemplified in the octagonal 'La Ronde' in Devon.*

*Left: Eighteenth-century houses in Philadelphia.*

*Top left: A Victorian cottage in Ockley, Surrey.*

*Top right: Dark red brick with pale stone quoins can produce a particular grandeur, as seen in London's Pall Mall.*

*Above left: The west front entrance of Hampton Court. Cardinal Wolsey began the work on the Palace in 1514.*

*Above right: A house in Aarhus, Denmark.*

## Brick

Bricks are small, uniform building blocks of clay mixed with sand and dried in the sun or, more commonly, fired in kilns, to increase their strength, durability and colour range. Their size is limited by weight to that which can be lifted with one hand. Modern bricks, which evolved from medieval Flemish ones, are standardized, easy to transport and to handle. Traditional brickmaking is a simple process, and bricklaying is a straightforward craft, although brickwork can be complex.

Good bricks are long lasting, weather- and fire-proof, and sometimes frost-proof. They are used for load-bearing walls, either to be visible or as a backing for face materials. They were also used as infill in old timber-framed houses; and today they are often used to face another material such as structural concrete. Bricks were traditionally used wherever clay was abundant, such as in low-lying areas or river valleys: around London, in the Lombardy plain, in the Tigris

and Euphrates plains, and in the Low Countries. Since the late nineteenth century, however, when new transport systems removed geographical ties, bricks have been chosen according to taste and budget and often without reference to local tradition. In the last century, sand, lime and concrete bricks came into use, but clay is still favoured as the more stable material, less likely to crack through shrinkage. Their cost ranges from cheap, machined 'commons' for internal walls and backing bricks, to expensive, hand-made facing bricks. Throughout history, brick has been considered humble or prestigious, according to current technology, economics and fashion: the term 'red-brick' may be used disparagingly, to denote post-war provincial British universities, in contrast to the stone of the older universities, even though many English mansions and French châteaux are also built of red brick.

In ancient times bricks were used by the Baby-lonians, who made rough sun-dried structures faced

*This Edwardian apartment building in London's Mayfair epitomizes the formally decorative beauty of brick.*

with kiln-fired bricks glazed in various colours, and by the Assyrians, who faced rough brickwork with carved alabaster slabs. The Romans also faced rough brick with stone slabs as well as using brick for facework. They made large, thin, flat bricks, or 'wall tiles' in Britain, but the technique disappeared until the late Middle Ages, during which time timber, mud and stone houses were built.

On the Continent, bricks became popular again in the eleventh century. Flanders was a major source of bricks, which were also exported, as ballast, to England, Ireland, and, later, even America. Dutch Renaissance red brickwork, with its crisp simplicity, influenced England and America. During the Renaissance, brickwork was much in use, either as a facing in its own right or combined with or faced with stone. Hampton Court, and East Barsham Manor House, Norfolk, are examples of early English Renaissance brickwork.

During the seventeenth century, bricks were used with exquisite finesse by Christopher Wren, and eighteenth-century Georgian houses reinterpreted

Classical themes in brickwork, with distinctive rubbed-brick arches over windows and doors. Brick was also a favourite material of the Victorians, and it is equally accepted in modern architecture, whether as a structural or a facing material, or rendered to simulate concrete. Being the basic cheap staple material in many parts of the world, it has been adapted to fit into the pattern of evolving architectural thought, even though some of those evolutions may have been stimulated by the qualities of other materials.

The appearance and appeal of brickwork depend on scale, colour, texture, bonding, mortar and contrast. Used on a domestic scale, brickwork is almost always pleasing, though huge brick apartment blocks can lack charm. Brick colour is determined by the minerals, such as iron, lime or sulphur, found in the clay; the method, temperature and length of firing; and the additives, such as sand, used. Bricks can be white, black, or shades of yellow, orange, red, blue, purple, brown or grey. Slight variations in their natural colour often make the resulting brickwork more

*Top left: A late eighteenth-century Victorian 'Gothick' cottage in Northamptonshire.*

*Top right: A house in Schleswig-Holstein, Germany.*

*Above left: This Victorian terraced house in Reading, Berkshire makes use of ornamental coloured glazed brick.*

*Above right: in London's Hampstead Garden Suburb, a model development built in the 1930s, brick was used for its clean lines and versatility.*

stretchers have a long side visible. (A closer, or half header, is sometimes used to complete patterns.) Traditional English bond is found in 225mm (9in) thick brickwork, with alternating courses of all headers and all stretchers. Flemish bond, introduced into England in the seventeenth century, has alternating headers and stretchers in each course. English garden wall bond has three rows of stretchers between each row of headers; Chinese bond resembles Flemish bond, but uses the 110mm (4½in) face. In the eighteenth century, header bond was popular, but today stretcher bond is most common, because of the almost universal use of cavity walls.

The mortar mix, thickness, colour and pointing all affect brickwork's appearance. Soft lime mortar has now largely been replaced by stronger mortars, of cement and lime or cement and plasticizers. These mortars can look and be unyielding, and lead to serious cracking. The general rule is that the mortar should be no stronger than the brick itself. Pigments can be added to mortar to mimic or contrast with the brick colour. Different kinds of pointing – flush, struck weathered, bucket-handle or square recessed – can create shadows and depth, and either a soft or a hard look.

Contrasting brickwork has long been used ornamentally. The Byzantines had decorative brick patterns and bandings, including diagonal and herringbone bonds. German Romanesque houses featured coloured brickwork. In medieval times, and later in the Victorian period, chequerboard and diaper patterns were popular as inbuilt ornamentation, while in the high Victorian period, brickwork was often a glorious mixture of colours and patterns.

Bricks combine well with other materials. In Renaissance Italy, Belgium and France, brick was combined with stone; in Moorish Spain, Renaissance brickwork was bonded with stone. Between 1784 and 1850 a brick tax in England resulted in many timber-framed houses having low-level brick and a tile-hung upper storey.

Bricks can be carved or moulded to form flat relief patterns or more three-dimensional sculptures. Renaissance houses featured moulded ornamental brickwork and terracotta, and although this tradition petered out in the early eighteenth century, when it was replaced by stone and stucco, it was revived in late Victorian times.

In America, hand-made bricks were used from the time of the early settlers, especially in cities and on southern plantations. American Georgian homes often featured rose or salmon-coloured brick, in Flemish or English bond, with wide joints of white lime mortar; urban houses in the Federal period (1790–1820) that followed also featured brickwork, especially Flemish bond. During the Greek Revival (1820–60), brick houses were trimmed with square-cut stone; in the Victorian Italianate and Romanesque styles, brick was often faced with stucco, for a smooth stone-like appearance. American 'Queen Anne' style, like its English counterpart, used brick in various combinations with wood, stucco and stone, combinations that continue to be used in suburban 'tract' housing today.

pleasing to the eye than using only uniformly even-toned bricks.

There is a long tradition in ornamentally glazed brickwork. Vitreous glazes can be almost any colour; plain glazed bricks are popular for decorative facing, especially in America and Holland, while white-glazed brick is used for reflecting light in light-wells in all parts of the world.

Bricks can be smooth; fine-, medium- or coarse-grained; sand-faced; sand-creased; grit-particled, stippled or combed; vertically or horizontally dragged; salt-glazed or vitreous-enamelled. Hand-made bricks often have a pleasant uneven texture, whereas hard-surfaced bricks, with machined edges, tend to have little appeal (though hard engineering bricks do make crisp details, such as copings).

Bonding is the bricklaying process in which each brick is lapped over its neighbour to 'bond' the individual bricks into a monolithic structure. The repeating patterns of courses and vertical joints provide the distinguishing characteristic of brickwork. Header bricks have one end visible on the wall face;

## Metals

Long before it became a building material, iron was made into tools and weapons. Cast iron is poured liquid into a mould, and when it solidifies becomes inflexible, brittle and hard; wrought iron is shaped when plastic, and is tough and malleable. Iron window bars and balconies were features of medieval and Renaissance houses, and wrought iron formed the decorative ornamentation of Georgian and, later, Regency houses. Cast iron largely replaced wrought iron in the early nineteenth century; relatively cheap to mass-produce in elaborate forms, it could mimic wrought iron, stone or even bamboo. The Victorians exploited its chameleon-like quality for decoration, and used it structurally: in England, for much railway architecture and warehouses; and in America, as frameworks for early skyscrapers. Victorian advances in cast iron manufacture revolutionized the construction of conservatories, eliminating the need for glass overlaps and heavy structural members. Large cast-iron plates were also used as cladding for factories and offices. The Arts and Crafts Movement, in its quest for the hand-crafted, reintroduced wrought iron, and it was also used to make objects in the art nouveau style.

In the 1880s steel began to be used to replace iron structural supports. Steel is a malleable alloy of iron and carbon, plus other metals, tempered to various degrees of hardness. It was made possible by the Bessemer process, invented in 1856, and one of the major innovations of the Industrial Revolution. Steel is quick to erect, universally available and hugely strong in relation to its weight. It was first used in housing after World War I, in an early attempt at factory-made houses; and again, during World War II, several houses were designed for mass-production, notably the British Iron and Steel Federation House, not only steel-framed but faced in steel sheeting, with a corrugated steel roof. While these were justified at the time by the shortage of houses and of craftsmen to build them by traditional methods, steel housing is not economical on a long-term basis, because of the high cost of the material and its anti-corrosion treatment, and the insulation needed.

The aesthetic exploitation of steel, celebrating its tensile qualities, was left for exploration in individual private houses, often built for the architects themselves, and involved partnering steel with glass. An early, precocious example of a house featuring naked steel is the Maison de Verre (1928–9) in Paris, by Pierre Chareau, while the purest expression of a steel-framed house is Philip Johnson's Glass House in New Canaan, Connecticut. Mies van der Rohe was the foremost architect to derive a style from the detailing of steelwork. His Lakeshore Drive Apartments in Chicago was one of the prime monuments of the fifties. Interestingly, the paradox of such a multi-storeyed steel-framed apartment house is that the actual steel structure must be cased in fireproof material; the visible steel is largely decorative.

*The Yacht House in the New Forest, Hampshire was built in the early 1980s almost entirely from yachting materials, including aluminium frames.*

*The Heidi Weber Haus in Zurich, Switzerland was an early commission for Le Corbusier and exemplifies his highly influential use of modern materials and forms, and his oft-quoted epigram that 'a house is a machine for living in'.*

*Marina City in Chicago—true home of the 'skyscraper'—is a fine example of the bold and unusual forms allowed by the use of steel-frame and concrete structures with glass walling.*

## Concrete

Concrete is a composite material consisting of an aggregate of broken stone mixed with sand, cement and water. Fluid and plastic when wet, hard and strong when dry, wet concrete is poured into temporary or permanent moulds, or sprayed on to a reinforcing framework, where it sets. Both mass concrete and concrete reinforced with steel bars may be either poured *in situ* or pre-cast and delivered to the site in units of various sizes and shapes. Blocks may be structural or only for facing, and beams, lintels and paving stones may also be of pre-cast concrete. Unlike iron, steel and timber, concrete is little affected by fire, and can be exposed to the weather.

The special properties of concrete were first discovered by the Romans, who mixed small stones or quarry waste with sandy soil and lime. It was used in foundations, domes, vaults and walls, the latter faced in stone, brick or terracotta. Not particular to one locality, the use of concrete extended to all parts of the Roman Empire; the technique was continued by the Byzantines in the former Eastern Roman Empire, but soon died out elsewhere.

Coade stone, a composite stone used only for ornamental effects such as rustication and door surrounds, was invented in England in the late eighteenth century, but concrete as known today was first used in about 1820, mainly for industrial or commercial buildings. In 1867 a French market gardener patented his idea of reinforcing concrete with metal – concrete in compression combined with steel in tension – to construct thin-sided flower tubs. This development, together with iron and steel, helped pave the way for modern architecture. Reinforced concrete frames are enormously strong, and relieve walls of their load-bearing role, allowing high buildings with widely spaced, slender columns infilled with thin, transparent or opaque curtain walls. The use of iron, steel and concrete frames enables large uninterrupted spaces to be created, forming the open plans of many factories, offices, stores and, on a smaller scale, houses. Concrete blocks are cheap, and can be composed to be light in weight with good heat insulation or, alternatively, be made dense, for structural strength. Building in concrete blocks requires less skilled labour than building in stone.

France is associated with the early use of reinforced concrete. Auguste Perret's apartment house at 25 rue Franklin in Paris (1903) is one of the first expressions of steel and concrete in the modern style, later brought to romantic fruition in the works of Le Corbusier. Other early proponents of the use of concrete

*Left: The Stephen David Erlich House in California's Hollywood Hills.*

*Below: A concrete building faced with stone in Amman, Jordan.*

in housing include the Austrian Adolphe Loos (1870–1933) and the German Walter Gropius (1883–1969), who later worked in England. There, the architect Maxwell Fry and the firm of Connell, Ward and Lucas used concrete openly as a modern material for housing. In America, Frank Lloyd Wright was associated with the innovative use of concrete blocks in housing; other early examples include the architect Rudolph Schindler's own house (1921–2) and the Philip Lovell House (1928) by Richard Neutra, both in Los Angeles.

Except in Mediterranean climates, plain, rough-surfaced concrete house façades often seem tawdry, and are therefore regarded as aesthetically unpleasing. For this reason, concrete used in housing is often rendered or faced in stone, brick or another material, which can then mimic almost any style. Exposed concrete is sometimes successfully used, however. Its appearance depends on the size and detailing of the units, if pre-cast; the size and colour of the aggregate, and any pigments added; and the pattern or texture on the shuttering, against which it is cast. Concrete can also be textured by hammering after it has set, as is done with stone; and pebbles or chippings can be pressed into the surface of the concrete once it is in place but before it sets hard.

*Left: This modern Australian house makes splendid use of glass brick walling.*

*Above left: An architect's metal and glass house in London's Hampstead, dating from the late 1970s.*

*Above right: This Hampstead house has very few solid internal walls, using the same type of large louvre blinds which screen the exterior glass to define interior spaces.*

## Glass

Glass is made by fusing sand with soda or potash, or both, and other minor ingredients. It possesses the seemingly miraculous properties of allowing outward vision and inward daylight while protecting against wind and rain. It is a poor insulator unless used in sealed units of two sheets, with a vacuum between. Normally glass is brittle, but toughened glass of various types is available for doors and large windows or floor-to-ceiling glass walls. Large-scale use of glass walls usually requires air conditioning or very carefully considered ventilation and shading systems, since solar gain can create intolerably high temperatures. Glass walls and blinds go together, for both shading and privacy – a particular challenge for houses using large amounts of glass.

The Romans made sheet glass, but it largely disappeared during medieval times when, for security, windows were few, small and high above ground. Cheaper alternatives to glass for windows included thin strips of bone, alabaster, oiled paper and cow placenta, which minimized light loss, and shutters, which excluded light. The glass used for churches or grand houses was blown and then spun, forming large flat discs. Small panes of window glass were cut from the outer part, while the thicker centre formed a 'bull's eye', the origin of 'olde worlde' bull's-eye windows today. Panes were set into latticed, cast lead slips, or cames, contained within larger frames – so-called 'leaded lights'.

In the sixteenth and seventeenth centuries, as glass became more freely available and defence less critical, low-level glazed windows became more common. Glazed windows were an integral part of Georgian housing, and during the seventeenth and eighteenth centuries, orangeries, the precursors of conservatories, were built all over Europe by the rich, to over-winter the then fashionable orange trees. Most glass at this time was greenish, uneven, and contained air bubbles and streaks. Better-quality 'crown' glass was expensive and only came in small sizes. In addition, glass duty, levied by the British government in the eighteenth and nineteenth centuries (affecting even its colonies) drastically restricted both its manufacture and use.

In 1833 methods of glass production were revolutionized, and good-quality glass in uniformly thin, flat sheets became available. In 1845 the glass tax was repealed, and relatively large plate-glass windows became a feature of Victorian homes.

Early buildings of the Modern Movement in architecture were associated with huge expanses of plate glass. Extreme examples include Philip Johnson's house in New Canaan, Connecticut, and Mies van der Rohe's Edith Farnsworth House (1946–50) and Lake Shore Drive Apartments (1948–51) in Chicago. The former, with its glass elevations and central opaque service core, depends on the surrounding woodlands for its privacy, and was not intended as a serious model for mass housing; the latter stipulated one curtain colour to be used in all the apartments, in order to create a uniform façade.

Glass lends itself to decorative use. Early windows in manor houses often incorporated heraldic crests made from glass of different colours, and decorative patterns and images can also be acid-embossed or sand-blasted on to the surface of clear glass (Victorian public bar glass is the high flowering of that art, and the ubiquitous frosted bathroom window is the mass-manufactured, functional version). Bevelling creates a more subtle form of ornamentation. Coloured glass was popular in Gothic, Victorian and art nouveau buildings, including houses, while reflective mirrored and smoked glass is less sympathetic to housing than to commercial development.

*Right: A colour-washed apartment building alongside the old port of Nice, in the South of France.*

*Below: The residents of London's Portobello Road delight in ringing the changes in exterior colour.*

## EXTERIOR COLOUR

Every house façade has colour. Even clear glass reveals curtain colour, the colour schemes of a room or the reflection of the sky or street opposite. Some colour juxtapositions arise directly from the structural materials, as in the wood and rendered infill of a Tudor house, or the brick quoins bordering the walls of a flint house. Other colour patterns are more wilfully decorative but still reflect the structure: columns contrasting with a main façade; red brick layered with pale stone courses in Dutch Renaissance houses; and the Victorian Gothic use of multicoloured masonry. All these are architectural uses of colour. Colour can also be superimposed to alter the sense of a structure, treating the façade as a blank canvas.

The Romans used marbles and mosaics for external colour on villas, and Islamic buildings were embellished with mosaic tiles and calligraphy. This tradition spread to Africa, where mud houses are decorated with rich geometric or organic patterns.

Medieval and Renaissance Italian houses were also richly decorated with multicoloured marbles, and

*Left top: A house on the waterfront at Key Biscayne in Florida.*

*Left middle: This house on Tortola in the British Virgin Islands shows the delightfully cool faded coloration prevalent in this region of the Caribbean.*

*Far left bottom: The islanders on Burano in Italy's Venice Lagoon probably use the same paint on both their houses and their boats.*

*Left middle bottom: A 'gingerbread house' in Martha's Vineyard, off the Connecticut coast. The term 'gingerbread' was originally used of showy painted decoration on ships.*

painted *trompe l'oeil* designs, imitating bronze or marble, were also popular. Venetian façades were among the earliest to be decoratively painted, and influenced much of Europe; Giorgione and Titian were two of the most well-known Venetian house painters.

In northern Europe, frescoes on houses sometimes depicted figures from Roman history, but, more usually, simpler decorative patterns were painted around windows and doors. Today, external house murals are a rarity in the Western world, although graffiti – art or disfigurement, according to aesthetic and social philosophy – is a recent urban phenomenon.

House colour can give information, for example differentiating between the part of a traditional farm building used by animals and that used by people, or to locate shelter in a lonely landscape, or to define ownership, by painting all houses belonging to a landowner one colour.

The earliest colours were earthy yellows, reds and browns made from natural pigments, and included

*Right: The market square in the ancient centre of Sweden's capital, Stockholm.*

*Far right: The Old Customs House in Colmar, in France's Alsace province, dates from the fifteenth century.*

yellow ochre, rust, raw umber, raw sienna, soot and ox blood. Heating these raw materials produced darker colours such as burnt umber and burnt sienna. In medieval times chemically processed colours were introduced, including rose madder from the plant *Rubia tinctorum*, cobalt blue from the element, yellow, white and red from lead, and various greens from copper. The eighteenth century saw the development of cheap Prussian and ultramarine blues, while in the nineteenth century bright colours based on chrome and coal tar largely replaced the earlier, more expensive colours.

White has always been an immensely popular house colour, acting as a focal point, whether for the whole façade or just for the front door. White rendering or whitewash is associated with a wide range of house styles, from rural cottages to houses in hot climates (where it reflects heat), to the houses of the Modern Movement. Many white façades now considered traditional were, however, originally a different colour: ancient Classical buildings were often painted intense colours; Regency terraces now painted white were

originally painted buff brown, to simulate stone: and American Georgian weatherboard houses were often bright blue, salmon, yellow or green.

The range of paint colours available today has never been greater, and there are no longer the constraints previously placed on choice by expense – many medieval colours were too costly to be used in large amounts – or by the sense of order given by local tradition. No longer does dung-coloured Norfolk wash, for example, tell you that you are in that particular part of England.

While paint is the quickest and easiest way to make a statement of taste and territorial possession, it demands careful thought and consideration for the larger setting. A detached house set in its own grounds and away from public view can be painted any colour, but the closer houses are, especially those in pairs or terraces conceived as a unified whole, the more important it is that colour is treated in a considered, and possibly unified, manner. The pleasing visual consistency achieved in vast sections of English Georgian, Regency and Victorian urban developments is often

due to the restrictions placed on tenants – even down to the colour of the door – by the estates owning the land.

Whether colour is to be historically correct is a matter of personal choice, although outstanding examples of particular house styles should be restored or maintained as closely as possible to the original. Modern external paints are available that precisely reproduce such old colours as rose madder, yellow orpiment (from arsenic trisulphide), and minium (from red lead). A painted façade needs regular maintenance, depending on exposure, paint and surface type, in order to keep its crisp, flat appearance.

Though generalities are risky, hot climates tend to have a light in which bright, intense exterior colours are appropriate. Given subdued light and grey skies, those same colours can look harsh or tawdry, and perhaps for this reason England is said to be a water-colour country. On the other hand, pale or subtle colours can look bleached out in brilliant sunlight.

## PERIOD EXTERIORS

Although architectural styles may be discussed in chronological order they do overlap, as more than one style tends to occur simultaneously. Different styles influence one another and are modified as they age or spread from their place of origin to other countries. Some, such as those of the Victorian age, are almost wholly derivative, plundering and reinterpreting numerous disparate styles. Others, such as the Classical Revival of Robert Adam, trace their origins more clearly back to a specific period. Others still are at least twice removed from their source: for example, American and Australian architectural heritage is largely British, and styles such as neo-Classical and neo-Gothic were first Anglicized before reaching their shores. A few – the primary style of the Modern Movement, for example – are genuinely innovative, derived from contemporary technology, materials and thought.

### The medieval period

The medieval period spanned a thousand years, from the fifth to the fifteenth centuries. After the fall of the Roman Empire, feudalism grew in response to the need for protection from marauders. It was the great age of fortified castles, which housed the lord and his family and, in time of peril, his vassals. Bishops' palaces rivalled cathedrals in splendour and, like castles, served public and private functions. As populations grew, small houses nestled around castle and monastery walls, creating medieval towns. The typical town house, built in local stone, timber or brick, might have on the ground floor a shop with mullioned windows opening on to the street, with a kitchen behind, and sleeping quarters above. As urban land grew more valuable, so tall, narrow houses, with upper storeys projecting over the street, became common.

In the country, peasant dwellings were largely of wattle and daub or had timber walls with thatched roofs. Halls inhabited by the landed gentry consisted at first of one large room in which the animals were kept, with a raised area at one end for the family and

*Oxburgh Hall in Norfolk was built about 1482 and has been the home of the Bedingfield family since then. Although substantially restored in the eighteenth and nineteenth centuries, its outward appearance is virtually unaltered.*

servants. This gradually developed into two adjacent buildings, or evolved into the H-plan manor house with a central living room, a kitchen at one end, and private rooms at the other. The cruck frame is a typical medieval structure, as are manor houses with steeply pitched roofs, many gables, and successive additions often resulting in an asymmetrical plan.

As well as the vernacular traditions used for most housing, western European medieval architecture also embraced the Romanesque and Gothic styles. The former, based on Roman architecture, prevailed from the ninth to the twelfth centuries, while Gothic,

named after less civilized Germanic invaders, was predominant from the thirteenth to the fifteenth centuries.

Romanesque style is marked by its use of thick walls, massive vaulting, square, octagonal or circular towers, and semicircular arches, often built in concentric, receding rings and supported on cylindrical, squat columns. Ornamentation was often lavish and was based on animal or plant forms. The buildings have a sturdy horizontality about them, compared to the elegant verticality of the Gothic style.

Gothic architecture features a high proportion of

*Above: A much-extended half-timbered cottage in Ockley, Surrey.*

*Left: The sixteenth-century Priest's House in Plymouth, Devon.*

glass window to wall, projecting buttresses, steep gables and, in domestic work, ornamental barge-boards, stone parapets, slender towers and an abundance of spires, pinnacles and ornate chimneys. The main characteristic is, however, the pointed arch. Ornamentation included stone tracery, stained-glass windows and carvings on doorways, windows and pinnacles.

Though largely associated today with church architecture, Romanesque and Gothic mansions and villas were also built, and, centuries later, Romanesque and Gothic revivals influenced ordinary domestic architecture. In America, for example, Victorian houses sporting towers with arched openings and ornamental arcades are direct descendants of the Romanesque, a style favoured by H. H. Richardson. The Glessner House, Chicago (1886–7) is typical Richardson Romanesque, with heavily textured masonry, a broad, overhanging roof, a heavy, low arch over the entrance, and a sense of weighty permanence. The Lyndhurst Mansion (1838) in Tarrytown, New York, is archetypal American Gothic Revival: a veritable pile of battlements, towers, gables and pointed arches, windows and loggias.

*The Ca' d'Oro (Golden House) in Venice, so called because its façade was originally extensively gilded, was built between 1425 and 1440.*

## The Renaissance

From the Latin for birth, the Renaissance refers to the rebirth of Classical Roman culture in Europe that marked the beginning of the modern world and the end of the Middle Ages. The Renaissance began in the fourteenth century in Italy, where the Gothic was never strongly rooted and where an undercurrent of the Classical tradition remained. It centred first on Florence, where the huge increase in secular wealth and power and relative political stability made conditions ripe for Classical scholarship, expressed in archaeology, art, literature and architecture. The writings of Dante, Petrarch and Boccaccio fostered new ideas, and wealthy noblemen such as the Medicis

provided patronage rivalling that of the Church. The invention of printing spread knowledge; the mariner's compass led to world-wide exploration and conquest, with wealth returning home to Europe. The Turkish capture of Constantinople in 1453 scattered its famous library and scholars throughout Europe, and many Classical Roman authors, including Vitruvius, were rediscovered.

Pure Renaissance architecture was based on regular order, symmetry and a central axis, with grandiose plans and impressive façades. Silhouettes were clean and simple, with flat roofs or domes replacing Gothic spires, though pairs of small spires were sometimes featured. Walls of large, dressed masonry blocks,

especially at lower levels, gave buildings an imposing sense of dignity and strength, harking directly back to Rome. Rustication – large blocks laid in courses with deep joints – was used with various textures: rough-hewn 'cyclopean'; 'frosted' (carved like icicles); smooth, with chamfered edges; carved with curved worm-shaped channels; and diamond-pointed, with each stone face sticking out like a pyramid. (Rustication can also be simulated in stucco, and was frequently used in Georgian architecture.)

Gothic verticality was replaced by an emphasis on horizontality, achieved with cornices, balustrades and balconies, together with stone or brick course-work with emphatic horizontal joints. Semicircular arches prevailed over doors and windows, and in free-standing arcades. In response to the Italian climate, windows were small and, in response to the fashion for symmetry, they were aligned vertically. Columns were used decoratively in façades and structurally in porticoes. Ornamentation of refined craftsmanship was based on pagan or Classical mythological subjects. External colour effects came from decorations in coloured plaster.

Alberti, an archetypal Renaissance man – architect, scholar, scientist, athlete, painter – wrote the first treatise on the Renaissance, and his buildings, and those of Brunelleschi, and, later, Palladio, exemplified the new style. It spread to France, Spain, Germany,

*The Horseshoe Stairs leading to the entrance of France's magnificent sixteenth-century Fontainebleau Palace, exquisitely situated in a large forest near Paris. King Philip the Good began work on the site, but the present building was initiated by Francis I.*

*The château of Azay-Le-Rideau in the Loire Valley, France. Begun in 1518, it was the first example of Renaissance architecture in the Touraine.*

Belgium, Holland and England, as artists, scholars and princes from all over Europe flocked to Italy, and Italian architects and builders were employed abroad. Each country developed its own interpretation, sometimes deviating far from the original. In France, for example, Renaissance style was amalgamated with the native Gothic architecture in the construction of country houses. In the Low Countries, too, Renaissance style was often applied as a thin surface decoration to buildings that were basically Gothic in structure and proportion. (Without the slave labour available to the Romans, the use of massive units was more difficult.) In Spain, the rich Moorish tradition was combined with that of the Renaissance. Early Renaissance architecture, refined and delicate, gradually became more robust and heavily ornamented, until by the late sixteenth century it had evolved into the – to some – over-robust, over-playful Baroque.

In England, the Renaissance influence was not felt until Elizabethan times. Elizabethan Renaissance house façades owed much to the Flemish, German Protestant and Huguenot craftsmen who sought religious refuge in this newly Protestant country. Elizabethan Renaissance style often incorporated much from earlier styles of building: mullioned windows, for example, and great halls. The Jacobean architecture that followed was even more affected by Renaissance ideas, but it was during the Georgian period that the architecture of the Renaissance flowered most fully in England, and led to one of the great periods of urban design.

America, not yet colonized during the Renaissance, absorbed the style via the filtration of English Palladianism. Eighteenth-century American Georgian façades reflect the symmetry and calm grandeur of the Renaissance; and it was one stylistic option among many revivals in the nineteenth century. The

so-called Second Empire Italianate style consisted of elaborate ornamentation: balustrades, repeating columns, and heavily decorated window and door surrounds. A Classical hierarchy of ceiling heights – progressively lower with each higher storey – was marked externally by horizontal courses. Fine examples include the Fifth Avenue brownstone mansions on New York and the country-cousin mansions on Dayton Street, Cincinatti, Ohio. The Villard Houses (1883–5) in New York, by McKim, Meade and White, and their Boston Public Library, reasserted the Renaissance theme, with its implication of refined culture and patronage of the arts and literature.

In Australia, Renaissance grandeur was made possible after the discovery of gold in 1851: Government House in Melbourne, modelled after Queen Victoria's Osborne House on the Isle of Wight, is splendidly Italianate.

*Osborne House, Queen Victoria's retreat on the Isle of Wight, was designed to Prince Albert's specifications in the Italianate Style and built by Thomas Cubitt in the 1840s. Queen Victoria died there in 1901.*

*Left: Hardwick Hall in Derbyshire was built in the 1590s by the Dowager Countess of Shrewsbury (Bess of Hardwick). It has an unusually large expanse of window for its period.*

*Below: The Hôtel-Dieu, Beaune in the heart of France's Burgundy country, was built as an infirmary in 1443 and served as such until as recently as 1971.*

## Tudor, Elizabethan and Jacobean styles

The Tudor period, from 1485 to 1558, began with the reign of the English sovereign Henry VII and included those of Henry VIII, Edward VI and Mary. Urban architecture at this time was characterized by mullioned windows, arched door frames and projecting upper storeys, and window glass was becoming more common. Chimneys were now being built as a matter of course in new buildings, and frequently added to existing ones.

Country houses were built largely by the newly rich gentry, who benefited from Henry VIII's sharing out of land following the dissolution of the monasteries, and whose homes declared their wealth. Houses such as Cowdray Castle in Midhurst, West Sussex, were often built round a central courtyard, on to which rooms entered directly. Moats, fortified entrances and battlements were still features, but now

*Above: The Merchant's House at Paycockes near Coggeshall, Essex dates from around 1500 and is an unusually fine example of brick and exposed timber construction with beautiful carved detail.*

*Right: The late fifteenth-century Little Moreton Hall in Cheshire is a classic example of 'magpie' Tudor.*

largely for ornament and heraldic display. Compton Wynyates in Warwickshire and Sutton Place near Guildford (home of the late J. Paul Getty) are famous examples. Craftsmen were imported to embellish royal residences such as Hampton Court, and formal gardens were created, in order to provide suitably impressive settings for the buildings.

In the Elizabethan period, from 1558 to 1603, the early influence of the Renaissance in Italy and the Low Countries – especially its fantastic, elegant decorative motifs – was felt and taken up enthusiastically by the *nouveaux riches*. Gothic features and basic structures were combined with newly popular, and often misapplied, Renaissance details. For the first time there was a shift in lavish building from ecclesiastical to domestic secular use. House façades became more and more intricate and irregular, with ornate chimneys, towers, balustrades and gables; and flat walls were enlivened by bay and corbelled windows.

During the Jacobean period, covering the reign of James I from 1603 to 1625, there was a continuation of the same architecture, with mansion building very much to the fore. Roman Classicism became more influential, however, both in the ornamentation and the preference for symmetry. Classical columns were used, and porches and entrances were especially ornate, perhaps even pedantic, in their display of Classicism. Windows were bigger than those of Elizabethan houses, and began to dominate the façade. Gables, whether curved in the popular Dutch style, or straight, were often featured. Hatfield House, Hertfordshire, and Holland House in Kensington, London, are typical Jacobean mansions. In America, Victorian Jacobean Revival houses, such as the Robert Machek House in Milwaukee, Wisconsin, sported decorative diagonal cross-bracing and ornately carved gables and door and window surrounds.

*Top: The Villa La Favorita in Vicenza, Italy is one of the many built in the area by Andrea Palladio in the mid-sixteenth century.*

*Above: The eighteenth-century Palladian bridge at Stowe, Buckinghamshire.*

*Right: The Italianate Style in Washington D.C.*

## The Palladian style

Andrea Palladio (1518–80) was a Renaissance Italian architect whose *Four Books of Architecture* set out in detail the Classical 'orders' – the Greek Doric, Ionic and Corinthian; and the Roman Tuscan and Composite – establishing in each one the proportions between the various architectural components. In 1715 an English translation, *The Architecture of A. Palladio*, was published, together with *Vitruvius Britannicus*, a compilation of British Classical architecture, by Colin Campbell. These books helped to popularize the style in Britain. A major early practitioner was Inigo Jones who, like many other architects, visited Italy to study first-hand the buildings of Palladio, which reinterpreted the Classical orders, and the Classical orders themselves.

The first English house built entirely in the Palladian manner was the Queen's House in Greenwich (1618–35), by Jones, who also designed Palladian stage sets for court masques. The popularity of the style was increased further by the Earl of Burlington, whose villa in Chiswick, now splendidly restored, is a direct copy of a Palladian villa. Burlington's influence resulted in the construction of many Palladian mansions, which were typically symmetrical and severely square or rectangular with stone porticoes, imposing central steps and roofs hidden behind parapets. Designed to impress, many had matching wings or pavilions, giving an extensive front façade. Most had one or two main storeys, excluding basements and dormer attic rooms. For the less wealthy professional and artisan classes, Palladian grandeur was more subdued, and was mixed with Dutch details popular at that time.

In America the Palladian tradition was adapted enthusiastically by the cultured and, by now, comfortable classes. Drayton Hall, in Charleston, South Carolina (1738), was the first example of Palladian style in America. Thomas Jefferson was a great admirer of the style, as can be seen from the original design of his house, Monticello, and in the Governor's Mansion in Richmond, Virginia.

## The Baroque

Baroque, from the French for misshapen, irregular or bizarre, refers to an exuberant, extravagant seventeenth-century development of the Classical in European art and architecture. The Italian sculptor Bernini and the Flemish painter Peter Paul Rubens embodied the monumental spirit of the Baroque in art, which began in Rome as a reaction against the staid Classicism of Palladio and Vitruvius. Freedom from stereotyped rules was the main tenet, and it was the architectural style adopted by the Jesuits.

It was in Italy, Austria and southern Germany that the Baroque was developed most fantastically, but it was also popular in the Netherlands, where a love of drama combined with a love of conspicuous display of wealth, and in Spain, from where it travelled to Latin America. Baroque had only a modest impact on American architecture, but much eighteenth-century American furniture and silver displayed Baroque exuberance.

Although less flamboyant in Britain than in central Europe, the Baroque, with its elaborate curves, scrolls and carved ornament, is associated in England with the work of Christopher Wren (1632–1723), and, in particular, with that of Nicholas Hawksmoor (1661–1736) and Sir John Vanbrugh (1664–1726). The dramatist and architect Vanbrugh designed Castle Howard and Blenheim Palace on the grandest domestic scale seen in England, and in the theatrical spirit.

In its extreme form, originality for its own sake and over-elaborate decorations resulted in designs now

considered cumbersome, unworkable or grotesque. Window positions, for example, were often determined solely by the appearance of the façade, not by the creation of comfortable living spaces. The Baroque style filtered down to middle-class dwellings in their use of columns with twisted shafts, heavily curved pediments and richly decorated doorways.

*Top: Blenheim Palace, Woodstock near Oxford, was built in the early eighteenth century by Queen Anne and Parliament as a gift of thanks to the first Duke of Marlborough for his victory over the French.*

*Above: A house in Zagorsk, Russia.*

*Left: Castle Howard in North Yorkshire, built for the 3rd Earl of Carlisle from 1700–1726.*

*The Circus in Bath, Avon, was one of the first of the gracious developments in the middle of the eighteenth century in this, then increasingly fashionable, spa town.*

## The Georgian period

This period, spanning the years 1714 to 1830, began with the ascent to the British throne of George I, and merged into the Regency style in the reign of George IV. The Georgian style is basically a continuation of Classical Palladian and thus of the Renaissance, with its emphasis on orders, proportion, rules of taste and dignity, but modified and refined. Robert Adam, for example, replaced ponderous Palladian details with fanciful, delicate ones that created a sense of movement, perhaps more noticeable in his interiors and furniture than on façades. Adam introduced Etruscan and Pompeian detail, and popularized the use of stucco, a form of plaster that was used as a

*Mount Vernon in Fairfax County, Virginia. The former home of George Washington, it was built in 1743 and was purchased for the nation as a monument in 1860.*

surfacing for walls and in mouldings for cornices and other decorative enrichments.

Georgian domestic architecture ranges from magnificent mansions, such as Adam's Stowe in Buckinghamshire, with its huge central, pedimented portico, symmetrical wings and flat skyline, to modest, simple cottages with Classical embellishment copied from pattern books by workmen. Most significantly, this was the time of the first large-scale terraces of plain and compact yet comfortable town houses, built for the new merchant classes. (Inigo Jones's Covent Garden Piazza of 1630, now demolished, was the first conceived of as several houses forming an organic whole.) Repeated, standardized units, rather than individual expression, became paramount. In the spa town of Bath, for example, elegant squares, crescents and entire streets were designed so that each house

*Left: An English country house betraying all the sense of proportion of the period.*

*Top right: Houses on Boston's historic Beacon Hill.*

*Above right: A splendidly preserved Colonial mansion in Washington D.C.'s Georgetown.*

contributed to the effect of the whole. Typical London houses of the period in Bloomsbury and elsewhere were built in stock brick, with their lower storeys faced in stucco which was worked to imitate stone. Windows expressed the hierarchy of the rooms within the house, so that the grandest windows were for the grandest rooms on the first floor, and they diminished in size towards the servants' quarters at the top. Semicircular fanlights were positioned over front doors, and very thin glazing bars gave an elegance to sash windows which were in other respects quite plain.

The Georgian period was the first great age of speculative building, with the landowner as speculator employing his own architects and builders. The English system of long leases reverting to the freeholder ensured that the landlord had an interest in maintaining high quality, since the houses eventually reverted to him or his descendants. It also ensured that terraces of houses built as an entity were not individually altered to the detriment of the whole.

Large Georgian country houses were often of brick and stone, with symmetrical façades, sash windows, columned doorways, bold cornices and hipped dormer or flat roofs. In London, the Mansion House and Apsley House, all in stone, were the urban equivalents.

In America, the Georgian style came to symbolize the end of the fight for survival in the new country, and the beginning of stability, permanence and the leisurely, dignified pursuit of culture. Georgian houses were built in New York, Boston, Philadelphia, Charleston and Williamsburg, as well as in the New England and mid-Atlantic countryside, and in the plantations in the Southern states. Though there were differences in the regional use of materials, American Georgian houses in the country tended to be square, with a central hall and external expressions of horizontality, while in the towns they were narrow and vertical, one room wide and two or more rooms deep. Both were consciously in the favoured style, with Classical porticoes, pavilions or pediments emphasizing the doorway, and eaves decorated with mouldings. As the style developed, ornamentation became less pronounced, more refined and more integrated into the structure.

The Georgian house was regarded as supremely pleasant, gracious and comfortable, and is still held in high esteem, to judge by the recent restoration of many urban Georgian houses that fell into decay or disrepair, and also by the neo-Georgian revival of the thirties and by the popularity of neo-Georgian speculative building of recent years. Today, however, the elements of the style are often used to create a tawdry architecture, with a few Georgian symbols tacked on to standard brick boxes.

*A house in Sidmouth,
Devon.*

*Classic Regency ironwork
on a house in Bath, Avon.*

## Regency style

Regency style (1811–37) is named after the British
Prince Regent, later George IV, whose favourite architect, John Nash (1752–1835), stamped his own brand
of Classicism on the period. Though a continuation of
Georgian architecture, it is particularly noted for the
stuccoed urban terraces laid out in squares and
crescents, often to a far-reaching master plan. It
obeyed the same Classical Georgian rules of proportion, and had the same relationship of doors and
windows to wall surface. Like Georgian, much large-
scale Regency work was built as speculative
development.

Regency style, however, was less rigid in its adher-
ence to Classical orders. Roman details were mixed
with Greek, Egyptian and Etruscan ones, to the horror
of contemporary purists, but to the delight of the
newly rich, who bought the houses. Although the
detailing is less robust than Georgian, the Regency
style often has a larger-than-life theatricality: terraces
designed to look like one huge palace had the central
house mimicking a grand entrance and huge porticoes and columns adding to the splendour. Regent's
Park in London, the spa town of Cheltenham and the
seaside resorts of Brighton and Hove are classic
examples.

More modest and endearing Regency houses
include English suburban villas, rectories and country
houses, and small terraces. Often half stuccoed, with

gently curving bow fronts or windows, curved, sheet-metal roofs and lacy cast ironwork balconies, trellises and railings, their human scale and charm are more likely to be a source of inspiration today.

The most eccentric and least copied offshoot of the Regency style was the bastardized Oriental, a mix of Indian and Chinese, epitomized by John Nash's Royal Pavilion (1824) in Brighton, a spun-sugar concoction of minarets, domes and fanciful ornamentation.

In America, the delicate ironwork verandahs and classic proportions of New Orleans homes are Regency in style, and chinoiserie became quite fashionable there. In Sydney, Australia, the Elizabeth Bay House (1832) by John Verge, is an example of graceful Regency architecture.

## The Greek Revival

While Roman architecture continued to influence medieval building and was the basis of the Renaissance, Greek architecture, with its more elegant if austere simplicity and minimal ornamentation, was largely ignored. From the 1750s, however, interest grew, and the Greek style was popularized in France by Claude-Nicholas Ledoux (1736–1806), and in England by Sir John Soane (1753–1837). The Greek Revival reached its height in the 1820s in Europe, and enormously influenced American building until the advent of the Civil War in 1861.

Greek Revival buildings are square or rectangular, sometimes flanked by smaller wings. Proportions are broad, details simple, façades symmetrical, and silhouettes bold. Free-standing or applied columns, supporting a pedimented gable or a flat entablature, are its hallmark. A portico may well emphasize the entrance, and pilasters with entablature may frame the door. White marble or other stone or white-painted stucco is traditional.

The Greek Revival style was much employed in Austria and Germany, and in England the arrival in 1801 of the Elgin Marbles from the Parthenon fired enthusiasm. The National Gallery and University College in London, and Grange Park, Hampshire, all by William Wilkins (1778–1839), are Greek Revival, which was one of the contestants in the Victorian 'Battle of the Styles'.

Perhaps more suited to civic than domestic buildings – much of Washington, D.C. is Greek Revival, as are countless American banks, courthouses, churches, state capitols and colleges – the style embodies grandeur, strength, timelessness and stability. It was also inherently aspirational, connecting the building's owner or occupier with the glory of ancient Greece. Nevertheless, in its heyday, Greek Revival also influenced house style, from the temple-mansions of the wealthy to nineteenth-century tenement buildings in France with Greek Revival columns on their facades. In America the Greek Revival came to be accepted as a national style, partly out of sympathy with the

*Cumberland Terrace in London's Regent Park, built in the early years of the nineteenth century by John Nash as the culmination of his grand scheme for Regent Street. Gracious terraces such as these were intended to stretch all the way from the Regent's residence in Carlton House Terrace in the Mall up Portland Place to the Park.*

*Right: Schloss Charlottenhof in Potsdam, Germany.*

*Below: The Owens-Thomas House in Savannah, Georgia was built in 1819.*

*Near right: A residence on Murray Boulevard, Charleston, South Carolina.*

*Far right: Built in San Francisco in 1901 for the timber-rich Vance family, this house was the only one of its kind to survive the 1906 earthquake. It acquired its distinctive coloration while under the ownership of the rock group Jefferson Starship.*

Greeks who, in 1821, rebelled against Turkish rule, reminding Americans of their own past, and partly fuelled by Byron's romantic poem, *Don Juan*. The Americans, too, considered themselves the spiritual heirs to the Greeks, who invented democracy. It was the favourite style of the antebellum South. The Lee Mansion in Virginia was given a Greek Revival facelift; Uncle Sam Plantation in Louisiana and Shamrock Plantation in Mississippi are pure Greek Revival. There are also outstanding examples in the Mid-West, in the mid-Atlantic states and in New England; Andalusia, in Pennsylvania was based on the Temple of Hephaestus in Athens. The style was applied with equal conviction to medium-sized and small houses, such as the Judge Wilson House in Ann Arbor, Michigan; and 'high stoop' terraced, or row, houses, in Savannah, Georgia.

Most Greek Revival columns in America are made of wood, showing that pragmatism and ingenuity could overcome geological limitations and scholastic purity. The style was also flexible enough to allow for regional variations in materials, so that buildings in the style could be of white-painted wood, or of any of a wide variety of stones such as granite, marble, sand-stone, fieldstone, limestone, cobblestone or even of brick.

## Victorian styles

Queen Victoria's name is attached collectively to a rich panoply of eclectic styles derived from many periods and cultures, and redefined to suit the tastes and theories prevalent during her reign (1837–1901). 'Picturesque' and 'Romantic' themes in literature and art affected architecture, and filtered down to even the humblest house façade. A 'battle of the styles' lasted for much of the period, with various forms of Gothic Revival and Classical architecture fighting it out. Morality reigned supreme, in theory if not in fact, and 'taste' became an emotive subject for debate. It was the great age of the self-conscious middle classes, whose homes reflected their wealth and bulged with the ever-uglier products of contemporary manufacture.

The Gothic Revival, originally promoted by Horace Walpole and exemplified by his house, Strawberry Hill (1760), was popularized by Sir Walter Scott. At first light-hearted and rich in literary allusions, it was later taken seriously as a true architecture of moral purpose – practised notably by Pugin and proselytized by the author and artist John Ruskin.

Gothic style was thought to embody the spirit of Christianity, and its intricate silhouettes and lofty, elongated spires gave a vaguely ecclesiastical air to all manner of buildings, as did the stained-glass windows. To many people, Gothic was synonymous with English, but late Victorian Gothic derived from the French and the Italian, notably Venetian, style. In contrast, Victorian Classicism soon developed from an early revival of elegant Greek detail into an architecture of richly decorative façades and the heavy look of Renaissance palazzos, as advocated by Charles Barry, designer of the Houses of Parliament in London. Later, Classicism was influenced by the French architecture of the Second Empire, with its high mansard roofs.

In Victorian times, huge country houses and London mansions, such as the now demolished Dorchester House on Park Lane, carried current architectural theories to an extreme. For the ordinary affluent and not-so-affluent, terraces continued to be built, in Renaissance Classical or French style, but people now preferred their own detached, miniaturized manor house, however close its neighbour. The coherent street façade lost out to personal territorial

*The characteristic extended ironwork canopies of the houses in London's Holland Park.*

*Above: 'Carpenter's Gothic', a Victorian house in Georgetown, Colorado.*

*Right: Victorian Gothic revival cottages in England's West Country.*

*Top: An 1875 house on Shelter Island, New York.*

*Above: Clapboard residences in the Victorian district of Savannah, Georgia.*

statements; working-class terraces sprouted tiers of angular bay windows, destroying the single, flat continuous surface so attractive in Georgian terraces. Typical Victorian house façades displayed an exuberant mixture of materials, and showed an abhorrence of plain surfaces or simple outlines and a general preference for asymmetry, seen as more 'picturesque' than symmetry.

Victorian house styles were international, travelling throughout the British Empire and also North America. Americans were particularly nostalgic, taking up European revival styles with enthusiasm. In the first half of the nineteenth century, the Greek Revival style was popular, first in Virginia, then spreading up through the New England states. From the mid-century onwards, the Picturesque, and especially the Italian Renaissance, Venetian Gothic and Swiss styles were popular. Andrew Jackson Downing, its chief proponent, was also one of the first architects to advocate the truthful use of materials, as opposed to the general nineteenth-century obsession of making materials appear different from what they were.

Towards the end of the century, the fashion for wooden houses, especially in suburban development,

temporarily eclipsed stone grandeur. H. H. Richardson's simple, low clapboard houses, with their shingled roofs, and the similarly straightforward houses of McKim, Mead and White are as admired today as when they were first built.

In Australia, early Victorian houses, nearly always single storey, tended to be of weatherboard, with a corrugated iron roof and sloping verandah. Materials and ornamentation grew grander, in time, but the preference for single-storey buildings with wide verandahs remained, due to cheap land, the constant exposure to wind and bright sunlight, and to the taste of the owners, many of whom had been officers serving in India. Two-storey houses, their balconies and verandahs heavily ornamented with cast-iron 'lacework', were built in the towns, and they hark directly back to the Regency style. Paddington, an inner suburb of Sydney, contains a wealth of such ironwork, locally called 'Paddington's lace'. After the discovery of gold in 1851, Australians, too, wanted to display their wealth. Anglicized Italianate mansions were the order of the day, often with square towers topped with iron railings. Vaucluse House in Sydney is a typically eclectic mix of Georgian, Tudor and Gothic.

## Arts and Crafts

This English Movement, emerging during the heyday of high-style Victorian eclecticism, was a reaction to the architecture embroiled in the 'battle of the styles'. William Morris (1834–96) led the revolt against the poor quality and design of the mass-produced goods of the Industrial Revolution, and sought a matching architecture derived from the natural use of materials rather than from an applied or enforced style. The movement took medieval times as its ideal, and advocated the return of the craftsman, with his integrity and traditional techniques. For Morris, the beauty of an object should reflect its use, and art became a metaphor for honesty and morality.

His own house, Red House (1860), designed by Philip Webb, began a new style in domestic architecture. It was based on idealized medieval architecture, but with Queen Anne windows, Gothic arches and a modern floor plan. The earliest garden suburb, Bedford Park in London, designed by R. Norman Shaw, a contemporary of Webb, took the best details from many styles – Tudor, William and Mary, Classical and Georgian – and presented them in new, practical combinations. This eclectic mixture of red brick,

Dutch gables and Classical ornamentation was called, rather fancifully, the 'Queen Anne' style.

One of the architects who worked on the Bedford Park development was Charles Voysey, whose emphasis on clean design, horizontal lines and the merging of a house with its setting had a powerful influence on modern architecture. The country houses designed by Voysey, Norman Shaw and, later, Edwin Lutyens, with their hand-crafted local materials and sensitive relationship to the landscape, were strongly influenced by the Arts and Crafts Movement and had profound effect on European thinking, leading indirectly to the birth of the Modern Movement.

In America, the Queen Anne style was hugely popular. 'Picturesque' houses were built that combined exuberant mixtures of terracotta, weatherboarding, shingle and stone. The open-plan bungalows built in southern California by the Greene brothers, Charles Sumner and Henry Mather Greene, reflected most clearly the goals and spirit of the English Arts and Crafts Movement. These houses were detailed and built with the precision of a cabinet-maker, and displayed a sensitive use of natural materials.

*Top left: One of Norman Shaw's splendid houses in the Bedford Park estate in London's Chiswick. Britain's first garden suburb, built to take advantage of existing trees and other natural features, it influenced all later similar developments in Britain and elsewhere.*

*Above: A perfect example of the English Victorian suburban house in Surrey.*

*Right: Otto Wagner's splendid Majolica House in Vienna, Austria.*

*Below: Antonio Gaudí's exuberant apartment buildings in Barcelona.*

*Above: A 1930s factory which architect Piers Gough converted into his home in the 1970s.*

## Art nouveau and art deco

Perhaps better known for its intricate crafts – Lalique jewellery, Tiffany stained glass – the art nouveau style also extended to houses. Art nouveau in America, France, Belgium and Britain, *Jugenstil* in Germany, and Modernism in Spain all referred to a style based on natural plant forms, usually using undulating, broken lines. A reaction against the frenzied eclecticism of High Victorian style, which combined as many historical periods as possible and jammed them willy-nilly on to house façades and into gardens and crowded parlours, art nouveau was a considered philosophy, and encouraged craftsmen to work with contemporary industry, mass-producing beautiful, high-quality domestic objects: delicate ironwork, wallpaper, furniture and textiles. In Belgium, the houses designed by Paul Hankar (1861–1901), such as 48 rue Defacqz, and Victor Horta, were influential throughout Europe, in treating the façade as well as the interior as an integrated, decorative whole.

A unique example of art nouveau housing is the Casa Mila in Barcelona. Antonio Gaudí (1852–1926), its Spanish architect and engineer, created the organic, fluid forms with a sound knowledge of structure, and the carved stone and wrought-iron decorations appear not to be imposed on the design, but to grow out of it. Originally ridiculed, Casa Mila is now recognized as outstandingly original, though Gaudí's

technique and extraordinary style died with him.

In Britain, Charles Rennie Mackintosh (1868–1928) was the most closely related practitioner, although the strength of his personal style also makes him unique. The Glasgow School of Art and the Willow Tea Rooms are his most famous buildings, but he also designed houses that reflected both the Arts and Crafts and art nouveau style.

Art deco took its name from the Paris Exposition Internationale des Arts Décoratifs et Industriels Modernes, held in 1925. Although art deco was a reaction against art nouveau, it, too, is associated with crafts and surface ornament in rich materials rather than with architecture; it also made use of the contribution of the craftsman and artist to buildings.

The sources of art deco are a curious mixture of the Wiener Werkstätte, the Vienna Workshops founded by the architect Josef Hoffmann around 1900, which continued the tradition of the Arts and Crafts Movement but accepted the machine as an essential design tool; Egyptian and Mayan decorative motifs; and German Expressionist painting and architecture. Strongly geometrical, with zigzags and curvilinear patterns typical, the style is exemplified by the Chrysler Building in New York. The stately London headquarters of the Royal Institute of British Architects in Portland Place is rich in its influence, especially in its fine interior detail.

## Modern architecture

Modern, from the Latin *modo*, meaning just now, is a moveable feast, since every successive style is theoretically modern until superseded by the next. Revival styles, such as twentieth-century mock Tudor, can be built with modern materials and techniques, but by calling a house modern one is generally associating it with the 'Modern Movement' – the conscious attempt by a group of architects at the beginning of this century to find an architecture tailored to modern life, and that celebrated new materials. Though influenced by the Arts and Crafts Movement in Britain, it first fully flowered in middle Europe, France and America, and during its early days was sometimes called 'The International Style'.

The Modern Movement, however, rejected the concept of applied style and the application of ornament for ornament's sake. It sought to promote and exploit modern materials – concrete, steel and glass – and to evolve an architecture more directly from construction methods. Interior and exterior form were conceived together and expressed as a single entity, and, with the exploitation of plate glass, the mingling of internal and external spaces became one of the main characteristics of the resulting houses.

Modern architecture was not just one more style but a fresh approach to design, reflecting and aiming to improve contemporary life. Private houses often became the testing ground for new ideas, and they were typically asymmetrical, cube-shaped and flat-roofed, with large windows in broad horizontal bands, or, later, floor-to-ceiling sliding glass doors. Mouldings were absent, and smooth white surfaces symbolized the proponents' celebration of sunlight and cleanliness. The exterior expressed, rather than concealed, the form of the interior. The placing of buildings in the landscape was approached with renewed sensitivity – to blend rather than to command, as had been the Classical tradition.

The Arts and Crafts Movement, with William Morris's philosophy and the houses of Philip Webb, Norman Shaw and Charles Voysey, was an early influence, in acknowledging the beauty of an object or building inherent in its practical form. Art nouveau's

*Above: The Crown Reach residential development on the Thames Embankment in London, near the Tate Gallery.*

*Left: A modern apartment building.*

conscious break with past architectural styles and acceptance of new materials and techniques was another influence.

The engineers of the early nineteenth century were another reference point. They had led the way in functional design, and revealed a new beauty in the bridges, railway stations, factories and market halls that were to be so characteristic of the Victorian era. Their works in cast iron and steel inspired those in the Modern Movement, who sought integrity in structure as the starting point for a new architecture.

In central Europe, architects associated with the development of the Modern Movement before and just after the start of World War I included the Frenchman Tony Garnier (1869–1958); the Austrian Josef Hoffmann (1870-1956); and the Germans Adolph Loos (1870–1933) and Walter Gropius (1883–1969). A prime contribution came from the Bauhaus, a German school of arts and crafts headed by Gropius from 1919 to 1928, which furthered the idea that artists, craftsmen and architects could work together on industrial design, and produce architecture which was unemotional, untheatrical, precise and logical. Just before World War II, many of those associated with the Bauhaus fled to England and later to America, where they were to influence a whole generation of young architects.

In America, perhaps by temperament more ready

*The Wachter Villa in Antwerp, Belgium.*

to accept change than European countries, Frank Lloyd Wright (1869–1959) evolved a personal version of modern architecture, particularly a domestic architecture, with houses and landscape merging. Hallmarks of his work were the use of indigenous materials, fluid, open internal plans, and walls as minimal screens. To the word 'integrity', much loved by the Modern architects, he added the word 'organic'.

A little later Le Corbusier (1887–1965), the Swiss-born architect and painter, contributed his own sculptural version of the Modern style with his apartment blocks and private houses. With his book *Vers une Architecture* and other writings, he became one of the principal propagandists for the cause.

Relatively few houses in the primary, or 'International', style were built before World War II, but the influence of these few was enormous. After the war, while copyists diluted the integrity of the Movement by playing with the various stylistic emblems of the early days, more serious proponents moved in several other directions. One route led to 'High Tech', and the use of tensile materials and glass, to the exclusion of almost everything else. While claiming to be the supreme functionalists, these architects can equally be called extreme romanticists. Another, more flexible route led to the use of modern and traditional materials side by side: brick and steel, stone and glass, pitched roofs and tensioned cable, which are all responsive to regional differences and personal styles.

In America, modern architecture formed only a small part of contemporary architecture: revival styles – Spanish, Dutch and English Colonial, Italian Renaissance, French Provincial and English Tudor – have always been more popular. More generally, twentieth-century house style in the Western world, whether Modern, revivalist or 'mixed breed', is a result of hugely increasing populations, a relative increase in wealth and the possibility of home ownership, combined with the shrinking social differences between rich and poor. These factors acted within increasingly industrialized economies and mass-produced building materials, the exploitation of prefabrication, the expense of skilled labour and a general preference for compact homes.

The negative aspects of modern housing – sprawling developments spoiling green landscapes; high-rise tower blocks unsuited to those forced to live in them; and featureless and characterless housing estates and developments – have many and complex causes. Among the most prominent were the need to house large populations quickly, especially after World War II; the new concept of civic responsibility for housing and increased land values, arising partly out of the wish to preserve the countryside; and profit. The huge areas of parkland, for example, that Le Corbusier intended as settings for his high-rise blocks, and saw as a necessary corollary to them, were frequently omitted because of urban land costs. Although architects did sometimes allow their exploratory enthusiasm to lead them in unrewarding directions, the worst housing was often designed to unrealistic or over-restrictive briefs, or designed not by architects but by builders, as a cost-cutting exercise by the developers.

*New housing in Saint Katherine's Dock, part of the planned redevelopment of London's dockland area as a new commercial and residential centre.*

## Post-modern style

Post-modern style is difficult to define precisely, but it represents a reaction during the late 1970s and 1980s against the moral rectitude of the Modern Movement, with its insistence that form follows function. Post-modernism is eclectic, borrowing historical details from several periods, but, unlike the true revivalist styles, does not attempt scholarly reproduction. Instead, Post-modernism is libertarian, a light-hearted, witty compilation of aesthetic symbols and details, often with arbitrary geometry, often unashamedly vulgar, and with intentional inconsistency of scale.

Private houses have always been used as a test bed for new architectural styles, and Charles Jencks, one of the principal initiators of the movement, designed his own house in West London in collaboration with Terry Farrell, and almost invented the style in doing so. In America, a precursor of Post-modernism is found in the Californian Locke House (1911) by John Hudson Thomas: its Italian arcades, Gothic buttresses, Classical tower and porch, and art deco ornamentation, are 'unified' by a rough stucco rendering in the 'Mission Revival' style.

Post-modernism has not yet entered the realm of general housing, because of its eccentricity and because it is much concerned with 'unnecessary' frills and ornamentation, incompatible with tight budgets or public finance.

*Architect Charles Jencks has made daring post-modern additions to his West London house which blend harmoniously with its Victorian character.*

# FOCUS
# ON
# DETAIL

The effect an exterior has on the beholder is as much a product of the innumerable range of decorative details that abound on even the simplest of buildings as it is influenced by the size, shape and design of the structure itself. Like the features of the face, their effect can be one of forbidding froideur, mysterious allure or warm and friendly welcome.

*Left: A front door in France.*
*Above: A window in*
*Lyndhurst, Tarrytown, New*
*York, dating from 1838.*

*An ancient cob wall in Devon.*

Like the clues that lead a detective to solve a mystery, every detail of a building reveals something of its story. From elements such as the shapes of windows, the ornamentation of a door, the texture of a wall, it is possible to create a picture of a building's past history. Styles and materials can sometimes date a structure quite accurately, or point to a time when it underwent alteration. Occasionally construction details enable the practised eye to deduce who the designer or builder was, or to pinpoint the source of features like stained glass or even bricks – all of which is invaluable knowledge for people concerned with the preservation of old buildings.

The detective work operates on another level, too. In more ephemeral details such as fittings and paint finishes, an exterior may reveal a great deal about the philosophy and attitudes of its present-day inhabitants. Accents such as plants can be used to enhance the colour and proportions of a façade, and there are other little touches that give a building a cared-for look. Thoughtfully chosen furnishings like lights and shutters that are appropriate for a particular style of house will also help to make the whole look a great

deal more than the sum of its parts.

The following pages focus in turn on the main areas where details count – walls and roofs, doorways, windows, plants and lighting. Information on the traditional and authentic treatments of these is given, along with many suggestions for cosmetic changes, and guidance on when it is worth seeking professional advice.

## WALLS: THE ROUGH AND THE SMOOTH

The walls play a large part in establishing a building's character. Their finish determines whether it is rough or smooth, homespun or sophisticated, whether it belongs organically in its environment or is a frankly artificial creation, a celebration of the builder's art.

Some house styles are inseparable from the materials in which they are made: the rounded contours of thatched cob cottages, for example, often seem to have emerged like mushrooms from the ground, and thick-walled adobe houses look like boulders baking in an arid landscape. At the other extreme are designs

that translate fluently into whatever material the builder finds to hand or the architect prescribes: the ordered symmetry of an eighteenth-century façade remains recognizable whether the walls are built in crisp ashlar (dressed stone blocks), the then newly fashionable stucco, well-laid brick or neat clapboarding. Similarly, High Victorian Gothic houses can be found in stone, stucco, brick and timber, with ornamentation in an appropriate companion material: fancy woodwork and ironwork with decorative stucco and terracotta for brick.

While roof or windows may vie for the honour in some designs, in most houses it is the walls that dominate the composition in terms of sheer area. Even where the wall surface is virtually a backdrop to an imposing array of door and window treatments, its colour impact needs to be taken into account when planning a scheme. The colour language of walls is largely a matter of texture. Take the different ways in which a wall might be red. The reddish tone of sun-baked earth is matt; reddish limewash has a glowing patina; gloss paint with a name like 'terracotta' masks a surface in a film of shrink-wrapping; reddish bricks

(especially old ones) weave their varying tones to give walls an infinite variety of lively, tweedy sorts of reddishness. The colour tones inherent in 'natural' building materials like wood and stone (and, in this sense, brick) make a vital starting point when you choose colour for other elements such as woodwork. With painted walls, on the other hand, colour shades can be manipulated and controlled far more freely.

Many wall finishes are covering up the structural material of a building. Some are the intended original finishes applied to disguise what was thought to be inferior, or unfashionable, or to provide vital weatherproofing, while others are later additions, perhaps disguising alterations in, say, brickwork to the shapes of door and window openings, or concealing new building in different materials where a roof has been raised or an extension built. The fashion pendulum swings between stripping back to the original finish and covering it up with new layers: as each building is an individual case, decisions of this sort are a matter for you and your expert advisers. The following discussion of different wall types is confined to the most common surface textures of house walls.

*Top: Traditional tracery wall decoration in Mauritania.*

*Above left: A window set in a dry stone wall in the Greek islands.*

*Above: Decorative brickwork on a house in England.*

*Top right: An ancient stone house in Hopton, Shropshire.*

*Right: The oriel window of a child's bedroom at the manor house of Lytes Cary in Somerset, parts of which date back as far as 1343.*

## Stone

Good-quality stone is a noble material, and to cover it up with anything is to insult its pedigree. Revel in its natural tones, and choose flattering colours for the woodwork, window treatments and nearby plants and plant accessories. If stone is dirty and not showing its true colours, it is possible to clean it, but take expert advice on how – and whether – such cleaning may be done.

Ashlar is often laid in courses with very fine joints. Rustication produces a 'rock-face' surface, sometimes used all over a building but more often confined to detailing such as quoins, or cornerstones. Of lesser quality are walls made from 'rubble' – stones more coarsely cut, their varying sizes accommodated by thicker and more irregular joints. Rubble is characteristic of cottages and less grand houses, but was sometimes used for the side and back walls of a house with an ashlar façade. Many people like to see rubble walls left in their natural state (well pointed, of course): since they are almost invariably built with local stone they can seem to belong to the landscape in a satisfying way. However, there are good precedents for colouring rubble walls with limewash. Unlike modern impervious paints, limewash allows stone to breathe, and affords a protective coating especially useful on soft stone. Reversing the process is also a possibility: old, flaking limewash can be scrubbed off with a stiff bristle brush and plenty of elbow grease. Take advice on removing other types of paint.

Local types of stone can produce stylistic curiosities, such as cottages built partly or largely of pebbles or flints. Brick or dressed stone is used for door and window surrounds where regularly shaped blocks

are a necessity, and would additionally be laid in strengthening courses, making a decorative contrast banding the walls. Where flint is 'knapped', or split, it presents a smooth, dark face; sometimes, in grander buildings, it was trimmed into regular blocks. Otherwise, like pebbles, rough flints produce a knobby, homespun texture. Since such houses already have pronounced colour and textural interest in the contrast between their tweedy wall mass and their neat brick, stone or render dressings, any woodwork and additional ornament needs to be neat and discreet.

*Left: Delforge House near Namur in Belgium was built in 1986.*

*Top: Decorative use of coloured bricks on the wall of a Victorian house in Reading, Berkshire.*

*Above: A terracotta panel on the porch of a nineteenth-century house in London's Belsize Avenue.*

## Brick

Because they depended on the local clay and on different conditions of firing, old bricks vary considerably in colour and texture, and even in size. Very old brick structures have an endearing irregularity and a lively character lacking in walls built since the advent of mass-production and standardized sizing. Until relatively recently there remained a great deal of subtle tonal variation between bricks; new bricks are now so reliably uniform that their cumulative effect can be a little flat and mechanical.

Most brickwork resolves itself into a predominant tone that suggests a potential harmonizing colour for the woodwork (if not black or white) or, at least, hints at colours to avoid. For example, yellowish tones of brick may look distinctly sickly with sappy greens and certain tones of red, while deep complementary blues help them to gleam positively. A good dull 'brick-red' brick, on the other hand, can be given a pleasing country character with mid-green woodwork, and often looks strong and glowing with a toning deep red or maroon paint.

*Right: Decorative diapered brickwork on the walls of The Vyne in Hampshire. This brick-and-stone Tudor mansion was built in the early years of the sixteenth century for Lord Sandys, one of King Henry VIII's chancellors.*

*Below: The entrance to a house built about 1660 in Abinger Hammer, Surrey.*

Colour and texture contrasts are sometimes already exploited in the raw fabric of brickwork. Some old walls are built in an attractive diaper weave, created by laying the bluish darker-coloured ends of the bricks (slightly vitrified as a result of the firing process) in a repeating pattern. It would be a pity to detract from the subtle patina of such surfaces by imposing an assertive colour scheme or by erecting eye-catching striped awnings. A more strident type of polychrome patterning adorns the fabric of many Gothic-influenced houses built in the second half of the last century, when bands and motifs were created from a palette of contrasting white, red, yellow and grey bricks. A sober variant might use terracotta panelling or rubbed or moulded bricks to add textural relief and patterning to the brick walls. Sometimes contrasting bricks are used more structurally, as quoins and architraves.

If you find it hard to match old bricks from the range of modern ones available, it is worth investigating the stocks of the architectural salvage companies. Some firms still hand-make bricks and fire them according to traditional methods. They can match the colour and dimensions of individual bricks for you, and will copy decorative terracotta mouldings, although they sometimes keep a stock of Victorian or reproduction moulds from which you may be able to find a close match. Remember that the way in which the pointing was originally done and the mortar colour are also factors in renovating brickwork.

Bricks have always varied in quality. Some walls were laid with durable 'facing brick', while other brickwork was intended to be plastered or limewashed. Experts generally dissuade people from painting bricks. Paint is almost impossible to remove without harming the surface; isolated paint treatment spoils the unity of a brick terrace; and paint on *good* bricks amounts to vandalism. But paint and plaster may be used to hide mismatched repairs and additions. On the flat uninspiring walls of a modern house made of perfectly regular, perfectly even-coloured bricks (already literally monotonous in effect), painted colour and a strong, interesting scheme could provide the salvation. Once it is begun, painting has to be repeated every five years or so, but you may consider this a small price to pay for gaining control over your house's appearance and imbuing a dull building with character.

*The house of Thomas Twining, the tea and coffee merchant, built for him in Twickenham, Middlesex in 1890.*

*A brick and plaster house in Montepulciano, Italy.*

## Plaster, stucco and cement render

From cob and adobe, via timber framing and second-class brick to modern concrete, breeze blocks and plasterboard, it has always been customary to hide some raw materials of construction behind protective and camouflaging coats of plaster or cement mixtures. Fashion dictates whether this should be rough or smooth, decorated, or finished in imitation of, say, stonework. It is a paradox that, while our ancestors used plaster and stucco to civilize the surface of the rude materials they were obliged to use, we roughen and texture the render we apply to our synthetic structures in homage to the supposed handiwork of earlier times.

**Lime plaster:** Before the advent of cement mixes, walls were usually coated with a 'weak' lime and sand plaster, often mixed with animal hair, to make a flexible layer that could withstand settling and movement of the material beneath it. This might be brick or stone, but was equally likely to be mud or some kind of timber framing. Infill panels in timber buildings often consist of either brick or wattle and daub – a sort of basketweave of timber strips covered with a mixture of clay, lime and straw, sometimes mixed with dung. The limewash finish that protected this plaster was often coloured with earth pigments, and it was sometimes applied over any exposed timber framing as well.

Modern synthetic paints may be too hard for use over this old plaster without cracking. If possible, continue the use of limewash, unless modern paint has already been successfully applied – which means that it will be difficult to remove. In this case it is best to carry on with the same treatment.

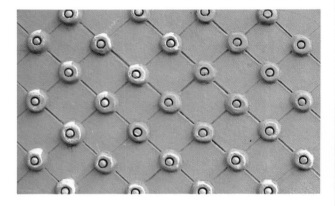

**Pargeting:** A decorative feature in which flat wet plaster has ornamental patterns scratched or moulded onto it. Pargeting textures some infill panels in houses where the timber framing is exposed. In buildings which have been plastered over, the lines of the timbers are simulated by a grid of plain plasterwork separating panels often pricked or combed into zigzag or basketweave all-over patterns. The visual effect is to break up large flat expanses of blank wall into pleasing proportions, and the texturing also helps to disguise any hair cracks caused by movement.

Occasionally, vigorous and fluid designs in strong relief remain from the seventeenth century, but many of the impressed pattern repeats on old houses today are Victorian renewals. Old pargeting worked in lime plaster tends to be less hard-edged and mechanical than patterns moulded in cement-based modern mixes, and its lines have often been further obscured by layers of limewash. New pargeting may be improved with repeated coats of paint to soften its sharp detailing. Unless modern paints have already been used, stick to limewash.

Good-quality old pargeting may be fragile, and cleaning and restoring it should not be done without expert advice. Where pargeting is being partially renewed or patched, the existing designs provide a pattern, and it is easy to copy original moulds. Always use a 'weak' lime and hair plaster (that is, one with no cement). If you are thinking of decorating a new building in traditional style, you could copy an old pattern or create a new mould in the spirit of the craft: consider whether you can incorporate some motif (such as a stylized rose or leaf) that reflects the name of the house, or has some symbolic meaning for your household.

**Stucco:** By the late eighteenth century, experimentation with different mixes (which might include stone and brick dust, sand, burnt limestone and clay and linseed oil among other ingredients) was beginning to produce some successful rendering materials that were harder and more durable than the old lime and sand plasters. These were seized upon by architects who favoured the Classical style for their ability to simulate the effects of fine ashlar stonework and be moulded into every kind of architectural form and ornament. With mixtures such as 'Roman cement' (based on hydraulic limes) it became possible to economize on materials and labour by building a shell in indifferent brickwork and yet produce a building whose façade at least possessed all the finest Classical features. Roman cement was succeeded by artificial cements including Portland cement, named because of its resemblance to Portland stone.

The naturally drab brown tone of early stucco, which was tinted with stone dust, rapidly deteriorated in the dirty atmosphere of the cities and it was often brightened with a coat of paint. It gradually became the norm to keep stucco buildings painted in off-white or cream, in homage to the admired types of stone.

*Above: Fifteenth-century houses in Saffron Walden, Essex, with pargeting added around 1676. In this ancient market town, named after the saffron crocus, the growing of which was its principal industry until the late eighteenth century, can be found some of the finest examples of this decorative art which flourished particularly in East Anglia.*

*Above left: Another fine example of pargeting on the wall of a house in Writtle, Essex.*

*Left: A house in Bath, Avon. A blend of stone and stucco, which has been very carefully marked and coloured to imitate the stone, gives a very pleasing effect.*

*Far left: An early stucco-fronted house in Australia.*

The all-over use of stucco fell into disfavour in the second half of the nineteenth century, precipitated by a boom in brickmaking and a philosophical revolt against the 'deception' of stucco's imitation of stone. Stucco remained useful for moulding window and door surrounds for buildings now proudly displaying their fabric of brick.

Today stucco is once again appreciated as a material in its own right. Because architects so often used stucco to unify a terrace or row, choice of paint in a bland stone-like colour may be a committee decision, with individuality finding expression only in the colour of the front door or other permitted accessories. Some places have a tradition of more exuberant colours, though: spa towns and seaside resorts (where frequent repainting affords important protection from salt) often sport houses in the pastel and poster palette of deckchair stripes. The traditional smoothness of stucco should be retained with gloss or semi-gloss paints rather than matt.

**Plaster and cement rendering:** Twentieth-century developments of rendering take two opposite directions. Architects at the end of the nineteenth century were inspired by a nostalgia for traditional building methods and materials, and occasionally used rough-cast plaster, usually white-painted, in their individualist 'vernacular' designs. The twentieth-century legacy of this fashion dictated the style of speculative suburban housing of the first decades of this century, often translated in Britain into 'Tudorbethan' half-timbering with roughcast cement rendering and pebble-dash. Pebble-dash was not intended to be

*Left: The wall of a house in the Old Plaka market in Athens, Greece.*

*Above: Detail above the courtyard windows at Little Moreton Hall in Cheshire, built between 1450 and 1580.*

*Right: Timber-frame and brick cottages in Limpsfield, Surrey.*

*Far right: The late sixteenth-century house of a wine grower in Riquewihr in France's Alsace province.*

painted, but – as with plain stucco – its often slightly dingy tones palled, and painting is now the norm. Unless a distinct colour is chosen, creams and pale buffs look more appropriate than stark white.

In complete contrast, the purity of smooth white-painted plaster and concrete became the hallmark of the Modern Movement and International Style.

## Exposed timber framing

The stout tracery of exposed timbers on medieval buildings inspired two schools of imitation in modern times, and there are broadly two schools of thought about how it should be decorated. Towards the end of the nineteenth century, architects experimenting with vernacular idioms occasionally used real oak beams in a reinterpretation of structural half-timbering. Along with their steeply gabled roofs and tile-hung porches, these distinguished houses might have projecting upper storeys of jettied construction in the old style. Far more common, however, was the pale imitation of half-timbering characteristic of the English suburban semi-detached. Debased to mere decoration, these softwood planks fixed to gables in arbitrary patterns had to be coloured and painted for protection, whereas oak can be allowed to weather naturally. Mocked for years as 'Tudorbethan', this kind of building is now somewhat more fondly regarded, even being granted the status of an architectural style in its own right in some circles.

Much timber framing in genuine old buildings was left in its natural state before the Victorian craze for

darkening it created an almost universal assumption that the magpie contrast of black and white prevalent in the wetter western areas of Britain was the authentic half-timbered look. Some blackening agents – tar, paint and stain – have sunk into the timber and are almost impossible to eradicate. Sandblasting and chemical strippers have limited effectiveness, and are not recommended for high-quality woodwork. Once painting has been done, there is a precedent for continuing the treatment.

A good deal of old timber framing was intended to be covered up, either with plaster or with a cladding such as wood or tiles. Another Victorian penchant was for laying it bare (much as we nowadays strip wood that was always meant to be painted), so that today's restorer may need expert advice to decide which of a building's previous incarnations to respect. Sound exposed timbers should need no treatment. The surface of new joinery or sandblasted old wood can be resuscitated with a clear seal, though the more laborious process of rubbing in a mix of turpentine and beeswax is infinitely preferable. Where wood has not been previously painted or stained, do not initiate the process.

Timber can successfully be limewashed at the same time as the plaster infill panels: if you brush the timbers along the grain before the limewash has dried, protective traces of lime will remain in the crevices to lighten the colour of the wood and reduce the degree of contrast with the plaster. Earth pigments such as ochres give limewash warm red and yellow tints, while vegetable dyes produce the subtle blues and greens characteristic of timbered houses in northern France.

Owners of Tudorbethan half-timbering have shared the dilemma of the purists: whether to emphasize contrast by staining or painting timbers black, or to treat them in the same way as the rendering. Untrammelled by historical precedent, the timber patterning on these houses offers an opportunity for new and individual colour schemes, perhaps taking inspiration from some of the adventurous and sophisticated combinations demonstrated by San Francisco's 'painted ladies'.

*Above: A sash window set into a clapboard wall in a mid-eighteenth-century house in Wethersfield, Connecticut.*

*Above right: The walls of a house in Ephrata, Pennsylvania.*

*Right: Weatherboard houses in Essex.*

## Weatherboard and clapboard

In areas where wood was in better supply than other building materials, it was customary to cover timber frames with horizontal boards. Timber cladding is a versatile material, capable of being refined and polite as in the fine Classical homes of New England, or rustic and homespun in the 'vernacular' style, and at almost any level of sophistication between these two extremes.

Originally hardwood was used. Oak, for instance, was split by cleaving. (Clapboard, used extensively in America, may owe its name to the cleft or cloven boards, though another derivation offered is the German *Klapholz*, meaning barrel stave.) The wedge-shaped oak boards were overlapped, the thicker lower edge protecting the 'feather', the thinner upper edge of the board beneath. Elm boards, which had to be laboriously sawn, were left with the protective 'waney edge' of bark overlapping the board below. The irregular effect was once considered appropriate only to farm buildings, but waney-edge boards (not necessarily of elm) are now used when a rustic finish is wanted for new houses.

The advent of plentiful supplies of softwood and, in the nineteenth century, of power saws, brought a trend for narrower boards with an even finish. A close weathertight fit was often achieved with shiplap or tongue-and-groove jointing. When painted white, the smooth fabric has an austere elegance that suits classical proportions, but also makes a good foil for decorative woodwork such as exuberantly carved barge-boards. With its quiet rhythm of horizontal shadows, it can suit both simple cottages and houses of more ambitious design.

Decorative effects include 'rustication' – grooving the boards in imitation of ashlar or bricklaying patterns, and shaping the lower edge in scalloped curves. By unobtrusively graduating the boards from wider at the bottom to narrower at the top, some builders

manage to create an illusion of increased height.

Hardwoods such as elm and cedar are sometimes not painted but left to weather to an attractive silver sheen. Rustic waney-edge board may be painted with creosote. Softwoods need to be painted, both to protect the wood and for the sake of appearance: sometimes the inside is tarred and the outside painted. Microporous acrylic and vinyl paints are recommended to allow the wood to breathe, but make sure that appropriate primers and undercoats are used. White, cream and grey are ubiquitous, but more striking colours such as ox blood are used with great success on American clapboard. You can achieve subtle, glowing effects by tinting paint yourself with earth pigments. You could add interest and enliven the surface of a wall by painting the boards in slightly varying tones – not in abruptly contrasting pyjama stripes, but in the softly modulating bleached shades of a woven rag rug. Another tactic seen in San Francisco is to paint boards in a subtle rainbow gradation of colours, from deep blue-green at the base through lighter greens to yellow and the orangey-reds of a sunset at the top.

## ROOFS AND THEIR DECORATION

A particular delight of hilly terrain is the way it enables you to enjoy roofscapes, from the crusty sunbaked pantiles of the Mediterranean, to old stone slates weighted down by colonizing mosses and lichens, or true slates glistening against a matching leaden sky. Time-honoured materials have a way of belonging in the landscape, and wherever possible they should be retained, repaired and used again because of their unmatched ability to convey atmosphere and character. Modern roofing materials almost invariably have a soulless, mechanical appearance compared with the items they are intended to imitate, although it is possible to encourage new replacement tiles to weather to match the existing old ones by painting them with a solution of organic matter such as cow dung.

While soundness must always come before appearance, it is possible to restore a roof efficiently and sympathetically, by respecting the lines and pitch of the roof as well as the materials, keeping dormers and gables in character, and perhaps enjoying some of the detailing listed below.

### Chimneys

On detached or semi-detached houses, chimneys are often part of the formal symmetry; in a terrace or row of houses built to the same design, the chimneys set up a satisfyingly regular rhythm. Altering the shape substantially or removing a chimney altogether risks destroying this overall pattern. (If a flue is not to be used, a ventilator can be fitted into the top of the pot.) An enormous number of different chimney-pot

*Top: A tiny but characterful skylight window set into a tile roof in Westleton, Suffolk.*

*Left: A colourful tiled roof in Crete.*

*Above: A shingle roof in Newport, Rhode Island.*

*Top right: A chimney stack dating from the 1850s on Somerleyton Hall, Suffolk.*

*Middle right: The arts of topiary and thatch in splendid combination.*

*Bottom right: A dovecot-type roof vent and weathervane in Connecticut.*

*Far right: Almshouses in Thaxted, Essex.*

designs were used for buildings until about fifty years ago, and they sometimes cluster atop a chimney stack like angels on the head of a pin. The Victorians in particular, who took advantage of cheap coal in the many fireplaces in their houses, were able to choose from a vast array of clayware pots and ingeniously designed metal cowls. Ornamentation in the nineteenth century attained an exuberance not seen since the barley-sugar and zigzag fantasies of Tudor brickwork chimneys.

If you have to replace an old chimney pot, it is often possible to match an existing one or to find a model so similar that the difference will not be noticeable from ground level. Not only are old chimney pots available from architectural salvage companies, but a number of manufacturers still produce new pots to traditional designs.

## Barge-boards

The practical purpose of barge-boards or verge-boards is to protect the exposed roof timbers at the gable end, and plain painted boards are often seen in this position. The practice of carving the softwood boards with curved and scalloped edges and lacy cut-out shapes emerged in the late eighteenth century in picturesque cottages, and became a keynote of the Victorian Gothic Revival, ornamenting the gables, dormers and porches that proliferated with that style and remained characteristic of houses built up to World War I. The curves and shapes in the barge-boards sometimes echo some other decorative line in the building, such as a band of shaped tiles, the ridging

pattern of thatch, or the curves of an arched window. Filigree patterning reached its apogee in the gingerbread decoration of American Carpenter Gothic. Ornate finials emphasize the angles of some gables.

It is vital to protect softwood barge-boards with paint. Strong contrast, such as white, lace-like against brick or tile-hung gable walls, brings their decorative impact into full play. On the other hand, a bold colour scheme, where barge-boards are painted to match other woodwork, can have a wonderfully strong, unifying effect on a building.

*Above left: A weathervane on livery stables at Johnsonville, Connecticut.*

*Above: Delightfully decorative barge-boards to match window detailing on an early eighteenth-century 'cottage ornée' in Old Warden, Bedfordshire.*

*A highly ornate wooden door on an eighteenth-century building in Aix-en-Provence, France.*

## DOORWAYS: THE FIRST IMPRESSION

The doorway is the key area of interest in a façade, not simply because it is the natural focal point but because it is usually the area offering the greatest scope for making your mark. It is on a human scale, for one thing, and accessible: you are not often able to do a great deal about personalizing your roof or even your walls, but the simplest door needs to be identified with the house name or number, at the very, least. If you live on a street where exuberant self-expression is discouraged, you still have a choice of paint colour as well as almost infinite subtleties of door fittings. Moreover, these are the details that evoke a response in visitors waiting at the door. The first impression from a distance is of the doorway overall, and the elaborate door surrounds created in the past attest to the importance of turning the simple act of arriving into a ceremonial occasion. Once you reach the door and press the bell there is a pause during which you can read the details to enable you to form an impression of what lies within.

*Above: The door of a farm
in Luberon, France.*

*Right: A door in
Mombasa, Kenya.*

## Doors in close-up

The earliest wooden doors were simple, homespun
affairs, usually a series of boards secured together.
They are still made like this today, where people are
using wood in the traditional form of planks to make
simple, functional rectangles.

Much more elaborate is the spectrum of framed
and panelled doors, with a great variety of refine-
ments. These are the 'front doors' that have been
designed and developed over the centuries with
deliberate care for self-conscious style and subtleties
of detail. They are formal, smooth, finished, civilized,
sophisticated. They are probably the most common
type, and what you can do to them is correspondingly
more varied. Moreover, their stylistic changes can be
minutely choreographed: something to take seriously
if you are concerned with period accuracy, or at least
interested in avoiding the worst solecisms of style.
And if not applicable to your own door, the awareness can help you appreciate and enjoy other people's.

A third category of door can be loosely termed
'modern': some of these claim classical antecedents,
but others are frankly synthetic, using up-to-date
materials in fresh and innovative styles.

The main scope for action on doors themselves
involves the surface – particularly the colours and
textures of paint – and the choice of door fittings.
You can also consider making some alteration to the
kind of glass used if the door or surround contains
some glazing.

**Board doors/planked doors:** Planked doors present
a simple, unpretentious face to the world. They prevailed everywhere until the eighteenth century when
panelled doors became more fashionable, and remain
the norm in unsophisticated country buildings. (They
also continued to be used for the unseen back entrances and outbuildings of stylish houses whose front
doors were panelled in the latest vogue.) Massive
noble originals of this genre can still be seen in some
old churches and ancient houses: they consist of
huge oak boards fixed to horizontal ledges with stout
nails and riveted to massive iron hinges. These structural details have, however, inspired a rash of black
blobs on many a frail modern imitation.

Planked doors are often referred to as 'ledged and
braced'. The upright timbers, often tongued and
grooved, are fixed to three horizontal ledges at the

back, and two diagonal braces stretch between these horizontal timbers and keep the rectangle of planks from distorting under its own weight. In today's doors, the vertical planks may be wide or narrow, sawn or planed. They are sometimes framed, particularly in ready-made new doors, which makes them less robust, more polite. Little one-pane lights may be let in to the top half at face height. Made to open horizontally in two parts, they become 'barn' doors.

These simple doors call for neat, straightforward accessories: a simply lettered nameboard; numbers in a no-nonsense face, perhaps enamelled; and traditional black door fittings (see later), and not too much of them. Massive black strap hinges and phalanx of studs representing 'olde-worlde' detailing are a pale imitation of the construction of the robust originals, and inappropriate on lightweight doors, whose hinges should in any case be on the inside.

If smoothly finished, these doors look good simply painted in one colour or varnished to match the rest of the woodwork of the building. The frame should also be painted the same colour, not picked out in something else. Use rich or soft colours (or black or white) rather than sharp, acid tones. An area of plain colour has a pleasing solidity of its own, and provides a cue for matching painted plant containers nearby.

A suitable alternative finish would be a distressed paint effect to imitate the faded, mellow result of weathering or the rougher-textured finish of un-planed wood. Dragging a coat of white matt paint over a base colour will soften that colour and bring out the rude rural charm of the door — white dragged over blue will produce a far-away mistiness.

The simplicity of parallel vertical planks also offers plenty of opportunity for naive painted decorations: for instance, naturalistic twining flower stems might echo real plants growing on the nearby walls; or a pair of motifs might be stencilled on either side of a window light, inspired perhaps by the cut-out motifs like hearts sometimes seen on shutters. You might even try a *trompe-l'oeil* window: a paper doily laid over a white-painted square and then stencilled in black creates a 'lace-curtain' effect within the window. One householder with no painterly talent turned a new, featureless door into a pencil box, each of the narrow boards painted a different colour, the sharpened wooden 'points' of the pencils painted in biscuit-coloured triangles against a black background.

*Above (clockwise from top left):*

*A door in Laguépie, South West France.*

*Armathwaite in Cumbria.*

*The stable door at seventeenth-century Saltram House in Devon.*

*A house in a Cyprus village.*

*The wooden door to a 1970s house in Tring, Hertfordshire.*

**Panelled doors:** Panelled doors (and their surrounds) sprang into being – in domestic architecture – as the deliberate and self-conscious design of architects who were influenced by the shapes and proportions of Classical buildings. From the seventeenth century, houses built by the fashionable and prosperous tended not to follow traditional styles and use local materials, but subscribed to architectural ideals of beauty and balance that became universal among 'polite' society throughout western Europe and North America. Variations occurred as different architects interpreted those ideal proportions in their own way, and because the designs were disseminated through pattern books and were further modified in the hands of local makers.

The standard front door for most of the houses built between the early eighteenth and mid-nineteenth centuries had six panels, although there were variations. This 'Queen Anne' or 'Georgian' style characteristically has a pair of smaller panels above four panels of approximately equal size. Such doors were often twice as high as they were wide, especially in narrow town terraces. Occasionally a vertical split gave an illusion of greater width. In earlier versions the panels were generally 'raised', with the panel surface on the same level as that of the frame and 'fielded', or bevelled; later panels were often flat. Door fittings consisted of a knob positioned centrally in the middle rail, and some variation on a ring knocker. These would usually be of cast iron, although more costly brass fittings were the choice of wealthier householders. Both materials are thus historically appropriate. Traditional paint colours included white lead, black and dark brown, but dignified deep shades of blue, green and red also suit doors of this period. Details such as the exact profile of the mouldings surrounding the panels and the way they were constructed belong to the realm of the buildings archaeologist. Anyone keen to restore or replace a door of this type should seek expert advice on authenticity; joinery catalogues exercise artistic licence when they list 'Classical' stock doors.

Four-panel doors appeared in the early decades of the nineteenth century and were used in most newly built houses for the next hundred years ('Victorian' is a shorthand description). The panels were recessed, with a longer pair in the upper half of the door and a smaller pair below them. By now wood was generally machine- rather than hand-sawn, which made the doors thicker and more substantial. Proportions varied: doors might be wider than before, and flanked by a narrow window on either side in a generously proportioned entrance-way. From the mid-century onwards patterned glass – stained or frosted – often replaced wood in the upper panels of the door and in adjacent windows. Door fittings became increasingly ornate, with designs for knockers based on Classical, Gothic and other inspirations. Letterboxes were often incorporated into the doors where mail deliveries were instigated in around the mid-century. Japanned cast iron continued to be popular, but cheaper brass became increasingly available after the 1850s. Grey, brown, black and cream were the most common paint colours, although more expensive deep shades of red and green were also used and occasionally clearer,

brighter hues. Mouldings around the panels were sometimes picked out in a lighter shade of the same colour. Brush-graining in imitation of good-quality wood was also popular.

The theme of glass and wood panels in various configurations continued in traditional doors into the

twentieth century. High-waisted doors of the first decades have deeply moulded vertical panels and glass in the upper segment, which might consist of a series of separate panels, domed at the top, or an oval containing a jaunty motif in stained glass. The art deco influence brought a hint of asymmetry, typified by a sunburst pattern of glazing bars, and sometimes a lower 'waistline' to accommodate a deeper area of glazing. Door hardware was chrome or painted black, and sometimes reflected deco lines. Bell pushes virtually displaced knockers by this time. Brush-graining continued to be a fashionable alternative to flat paint on panelled doors, and plain colours on external woodwork were often dark green or brown. Panels or mouldings, or both, were sometimes painted in a contrasting colour, just as windows sometimes teamed a deeper frame colour with a paler lining, such as chocolate brown with pale yellow or cream, dark green or Indian red with cream, or lighter green with yellow or buff.

Good-quality doors deserve good-quality paintwork, but unless you are bent on fidelity to period accuracy (something on which the experts are not always unanimous) you can usually choose colours outside the recommended ranges to good effect, particularly if they are part of a cohesive scheme – and they please you. For something different, consider graining: you can still buy ready-prepared graining paints that imitate tones of oak and so on, or you could consider a do-it-yourself version, varying the colours to suit yourself. Another way of personalizing your door is to exploit the panelling. The device of picking out mouldings is usually jumpy and fiddly,

*Above left: A grand Georgian doorway..*

*Above: A door in Winchelsea, East Sussex.*

*Right: A doorway in Oundle, Northamptonshire.*

*Above right (clockwise from top left):*

*An Autumnal Halloween display in Essex, Connecticut.*

*A door dating from the 1840s in the Clifton district of Bristol, Avon.*

*An ornate door in Norwich, Norfolk.*

*A door set into a flint wall in Brentwood, Middlesex.*

particularly when strong contrasts are chosen; a more subtle and harmonious approach is to use closely related tones, or to combine a distressed finish in the panels with the base colour used plain on the frame.

Damaged stained glass can usually be repaired by glaziers. If you are thinking of restoration or replacement, architectural salvage dealers stock various pieces of stained glass: in the building boom towards the end of the last century, and particularly in Britain with the proliferation of terraced houses earlier this century, designs for door panels and window lights were stock items, and it is possible to find something that has been salvaged from a similar building to your own. A number of firms and individuals make stained glass to order, but if you are considering this option, make sure that you see their work before you commit yourself. Some coloured glass offered by double-glazing firms in particular is a crude, synthetic imitation of the hand-made glass originally used.

If you want something to enliven a plain panel of glass and feel like tackling it yourself, use hobbyist cold-glass paints (which need no firing) from good crafts shops. The colours are garish in comparison with the mellow tones of true stained glass, but by experimenting with thinners and perhaps a limited palette of hues, you can create a glowing, translucent design on glass. You could separate areas of colour with heavy black lines like the leading in the real thing. If the result is a masterpiece, you will want to protect it from direct sunlight and from handling, but you could regard it as a cheap and cheerful temporary expedient, to be replaced one day by the genuine article when the budget allows.

**Modern styles:** The post-war revolt against the stylistic clutter of traditional mouldings and ornamentation produced a range of flush doors, plain and unadorned, inset to varying degrees with panels of textured plate glass. All the colours of the spectrum were now available in paint, including fashionable novelties such as purple and yellow. Door fittings in aluminium or zinc alloy were characterized by clean, streamlined shapes. The best of these doors are well proportioned and functionally elegant, but too many are both graceless and characterless. Sometimes it is the uninspiring texture of the frosted or rolled glass that makes these doors seem dated: replacing it with clear glass (backed if necessary with a lace curtain)

can provide just the right freshening touch.

Another type of modern door is one made of tropical hardwood, and supposedly a replica of a traditional design, usually reverently varnished to reveal glowing 'natural' colours. Some of these doors are suitable for new houses, but too often they are used on older buildings with stylistic detailing of their own which should be respected. These doors seem to retain their own identity rather than blending in with or complementing the house's façade.

The best way to integrate one of these doors into the façade of a house rather than leaving it as a raw status symbol is with paint. If you have a boldly coloured paint scheme unifying the woodwork of other parts of the house, treating the door in the same way diminishes its pretensions and makes it belong. Other options are to soften its effect with a distressed finish: try mock-oak graining for a tongue-in-cheek parody of a parody. A dragged finish on the door could be rich or gentle, depending on the tones used and the colour and texture of adjacent wall surfaces: it would withstand the competition of painted rendering, for example, better than the crisp and graphic grid of a new brick wall nearby.

While the challenge with the new-wave panelled doors is to make them less pompous, with plain flush doors you may want to introduce some character, even an element of fantasy. Consider painting *trompe l'oeil* panels and fielding, or try stencilling. Alternatively, use some ready-made mouldings available for plasterwork effects indoors: they should be permanent provided you stick them soundly to the door surface and protect them with exterior-grade paint. If you choose some of the more figurative swags or floral motifs, you can then have fun with paint, picking them out in naturalistic colours, perhaps, and finishing with a couple of coats of varnish.

*Opposite page: The Wychcombe studios in North London were built in the Victorian era to house artists. Extensive modern refurbishment included this elegant entrance to the pyramid conservatory room.*

*Top left: The glass door with glass-brick surround of a home converted from a warehouse in Princeton, New Jersey in the late 1970s.*

*Top right: The door to a 1930s English suburban house.*

*Above: Another 1930s door in Norwich, Norfolk.*

*Left: The dramatic glass door to a 1970s mews redevelopment in London's Holland Park.*

*Right (clockwise from top left):*

*Door handle on the mid-eighteenth century Pratt House, Essex, Connecticut.*

*Fittings on a wooden door in Ibiza, Spain.*

*A classic brass bell push in Germany.*

*Black-painted metal door fittings on an elegant English door.*

*Brass door fittings make a striking contrast on this blue-painted door on a Georgian house in Spitalfields, East London.*

*A cast-iron door knocker on a wooden panelled door in Bellème in Orne, France.*

## Fittings and accessories

A distinct period style is enhanced by appropriate fittings and accessories. Some doorways will have a character that you can go along with: a hint of art nouveau in the door's stained glass, for example, is a pretext for a knocker and letterplate in correspondingly fluid lines; a thirties door will look happier furnished in chrome than in a Regency brass design with beaded edges. Often, however, there is no such cue. If a door is plain and style-less, furnishing it with an assortment of knobs and paraphernalia does not necessarily create a style. On utilitarian doors a letterplate incorporating a handle that pulls the door shut and also serves as a knocker may look more streamlined than three separate items. Keep embellishments for the nameplate, and for plants or other decorative features nearby.

'Modern' doors in situations where you can cheerfully avoid historical precedent and stylistic constraint should offer a free hand. You can choose modern, streamlined fittings or refer to past styles and go for something more decorative. New 'Classical' or 'period' panelled doors are often fairly small in relation to the imposing porticoed entranceways of the past, so keep an eye on scale. A neat, simple version of (say) the Classical urn design or a compact lion's head might give just the right touch of dignity, but it is easy to overdo it. Manufacturers' catalogues tempt you to pick several items from one of their co-ordinated suites for a total look – handles, letterplate, bellpush, knocker, etc – but unless your door is very

grand, exercise restraint. Rare exceptions can carry off excess, but most doors are better dressed in more modest items, and fewer of them: too much brass or too many fiddly bits of iron can look tiresome. It is equally important to avoid mixing materials: an enamelled house number, a brass knocker, iron hinges and a painted nameplate simply look untidy. As with the design of door fittings – which can combine function and ornamentation in varying degrees – and of the number and/or name that identifies the house, give careful thought to any adjacent accessories that may contribute to the picture, including lights, door-mats, handrails and so on.

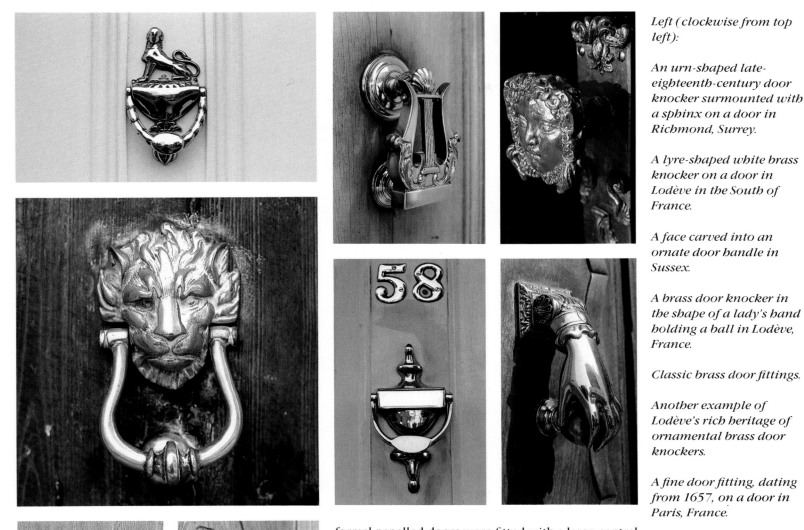

*Left (clockwise from top left):*

*An urn-shaped late-eighteenth-century door knocker surmounted with a sphinx on a door in Richmond, Surrey.*

*A lyre-shaped white brass knocker on a door in Lodève in the South of France.*

*A face carved into an ornate door handle in Sussex.*

*A brass door knocker in the shape of a lady's hand holding a ball in Lodève, France.*

*Classic brass door fittings.*

*Another example of Lodève's rich heritage of ornamental brass door knockers.*

*A fine door fitting, dating from 1657, on a door in Paris, France.*

*A decorative lion's head knocker on a door in Malta.*

**Handles and locks:** Two styles of domestic handle survive from the robust security systems of the old planked doors, and invariably suit their modern successors. A ring handle that turns to lift a latch is the more sophisticated option, while the thumblatch or Suffolk latch is in keeping with the simplicity of less refined cottage doors (depressing the thumb-plate set above a vertical handle raises the latch inside the door). Both these are traditionally of black-painted iron, and plenty of good-quality old designs are reproduced today.

With the development of brass, iron and finally steel locks, opened by a key inserted from the outside, formal panelled doors were fitted with a large central knob to pull them closed. Usually of iron rather than brass, these were often ornamental, perhaps with milled edges or in a 'Gothic' segmented design. In later doors the handle was positioned to one side and became incorporated in the lock mechanism. Levers now increasingly take the place of knobs.

**Doorknockers and bells:** Fantasists of the nineteenth century in particular made great play with doorknockers in the shape of animal masks, sphinx or Medusa heads, hands clutching wreaths, fists and other representational motifs which joined an array of Classical urns and straightforward rings and S-shapes. The range of designs available today — many of them reproductions from some two centuries of inspiration — offers plenty of choice, but if you are buying a reproduction, buy a good one. You may be lucky enough to find a design that works as a symbol, linked with your name or the name of your house; or some decorative motif or border that sets a theme for a broader decorative treatment. If yours is a house in a row or terrace much circumscribed by restrictions about door colours and styles of nameplate, choosing a rare and idiosyncratic knocker may be your one discreet means of self-advertisement.

Bell pulls came into use in the early 1800s and were superseded by electric doorbells around the turn of the century. Many of these were simple porcelain buttons, but some were mounted in handsome brass surrounds.

*Right ( this page, clockwise from top left):*

*A fine old example of the American mail box, with wire loops for newspapers, in Lititz, Pennsylvania.*

*A dated lintel stone in Falkland, Fife.*

*A hand-painted door in Nayland, Suffolk.*

*An 1815 ironwork boot-scraper in Priory Parade, one of the elegant terraces of houses in Cheltenham, Gloucestershire.*

*A boot-scraper set in the wall of a house in Burnham Market, Norfolk.*

*The plainest of door names can be given a different look from time to time, using the most inexpensive of accessories.*

*Rural mail boxes in Connecticut.*

*Left: Even the boldest of modern treatments can give scope for the personal touch.*

*Below: A carved wooden name-plate set in the gate-post of a house in Essex, Connecticut.*

**Letterboxes and mailboxes:** Although some householders have no such option, where the mail is delivered to the door the choice between a letterplate and a freestanding mailbox is sometimes useful. Many traditional doors have had a slot cut into them and look none the worse for it, but some designs offer no logical place for a letterbox. A mailbox attached to the wall or the side of the door opening can be either plain and understated or ornamented as a feature in its own right. Letterplates, too, can either be low-key or quite distinctive, making a contribution to the overall door style. Antiques and good reproductions from the last century abound; it is more difficult to find early twentieth-century ones in good condition.

**Names and numbers:** A Classical style of house calls for a dignified label, such as a brass plate with incised lettering. Slate is an alternative in an area with slate roofs or doorsteps. For house numbers, playing it straight means choosing well-designed figures in brass, black-finished iron or white enamel and screwing them to the wood of the door or gate. Painted figures in equally sober script, or French-style enamelled ones, are other possibilities. You can sometimes paint

the house name on a lintel above a door. Wrought-iron, wood (smooth or rustic) and painted porcelain plaques can all be effective in the appropriate context, and – as with hand-painted signs – you may be able to use ornamentation to play on the name of the house. Clarity and legibility are priorities, and this may be taken to extremes: on a mundane façade, cleverly painted outsize figures may contribute the missing individuality.

**Shoescrapers and doormats:** These can be the finishing touch or an irrelevance: it depends on whether they make sense at your doorstep. Doormats at least can be a necessity to prevent shoes from carrying deposits from a gritty tarmac straight indoors, just as iron bootscrapers were important when roads were muddy. You may find a designer doormat with just the right colour tones to flatter your front door, or a period 'welcome' or sunburst motif in keeping with the house's style. Otherwise keep a mat as simple as possible. A family that always travels by car can scarcely justify setting a cast-iron shoescraper outside the front door of their brand-new house, whereas country households might find them essential.

*Right (clockwise from top left):*

*A late eighteenth-century Federal-style door on Chestnut Street, Salem, Massachusetts.*

*A door in Mindelheim in Germany's Bavaria.*

*Another door in Mindelheim.*

*A Regency door in Priory Parade, Cheltenham, Gloucestershire. The ornate wrought-iron porch incorporates twin boot-scrapers.*

## Door surrounds

While an overhead projection may shelter a doorway from rain, other forms of ornamentation around doorways are there for appearance only, for the aggrandizement of the entranceway. Even the simplest kind of framing device on a flat façade, such as an architrave picked out with paint, increases the size and impact of the doorway. Attaching some form of three-dimensional structure is another option. Adding a canopy or portico was almost standard practice for some two centuries, until the simplicity ordained by the Modern Movement banished such accretions. Since the 1970s, as if in reaction to such austerity, not only have period features been appreciated and restored, but new houses are often built with ornate doorways that hark back to Classical inspiration. In more modest dwellings built during the last hundred years, door surrounds (like the doors themselves) are threatened by many owners' desire to add some form of double-glazing to the façade. Sometimes the lines of the original front door are preserved beneath the glass as if in aspic; in other cases ingenious adaptations have changed the original shape beyond recognition.

**'Classical' door treatments:** As with the panelled doors of the period, it was in the eighteenth century that the aesthetic rules concerning door surrounds were formulated in exquisite detail. Appealing to Classical models, architects designed columns, pilasters, pediments and so on according to strictly elaborated theories of proportion. Over the door was the horizontal entablature, above which might rise a triangular or curved pediment. The entablature might be supported by a pair of ornamental brackets or consoles, but was very often based on a pair of pilasters or columns flanking the door. The formal composition of these according to, first, Roman and, later, Greek orders of architecture was the subject of much study. The important thing is that the doorway was designed as a whole, with total attention to the overall proportion and harmony of the façade. Builders constructed these elements from whatever materials were locally available: timber, stone or brick and stucco. Generally they were painted in off-white or pale buff tones to imitate stone.

Some of these ideals persisted in the nineteenth century and influenced grander schemes, but many

*Left (clockwise from top left):*

*A red door set in an elaborate classical surround.*

*A sober door in Church Row in London's Hampstead, painted green with a wide white glazed surround.*

*The rural idyll in Overbury, Gloucestershire.*

*An ornate fifteenth-century door in Viterbo, Italy.*

*A white-painted Georgian door in Burnham Market, Norfolk. The, now uncommon, small iron gate immediately in front allowed the door to be left open in summer while keeping children and dogs safe.*

*A decoratively painted door in Denmark's Jutland.*

more were either bastardized versions of the Classical ones, or took inspiration from elsewhere: Egypt, the Gothic, Arts and Crafts, or a nostalgia for rural 'vernacular'. These last influenced the design of buildings until World War II.

An authentic period surround is something to be treasured, and any restoration work should be carried out with expert advice. Restoration is almost invariably preferable to replacement, unless extremely accurate replicas can be obtained. Fibreglass is occasionally possible for old buildings (and to be used only with professional advice), but full of potential if you are starting from scratch and do not need to match or integrate new elements with originals. Manufacturers' catalogues show a range of elements – including columns, pilasters and entablatures – from which you can build up the complete door surround of your choice. Occasionally this may result in something approximating to the Classical proportions, but beware of the disregard for overall system implicit in the jigsaw principle and such conveniences as the facility of cutting the bases of pilasters or columns to fit the actual dimensions on site.

Where there is no historical precedent to take seriously, you can have fun borrowing these elements and building your own grand entrance. One reason for their trivial, fiddly appearance on some pretentious modern houses lies in the finish, a smooth white gloss adding to their insubstantial quality. In the eighteenth century the various materials used were finished to look like stone, and a modern masonry paint that adds a more textured solidity will help to reduce that new, ersatz look. Alternatively, take an even more irreverent approach and use colour. As part of a boldly engineered scheme, a mock-Classical portico in (say) deep blue moves into a class of its own. As with pseudo-characterful modern hardwood doors, colour has a dignifying and ennobling effect.

If you are considering adding a portico on Classical lines, you may not wish to go to eighteenth-century lengths, but do think about the overall proportions. Many of the more splendid treatments were designed for houses built on a far grander scale than that of most homes today, and a door surround that dwarfs the façade instead of adding grandeur is worse than nothing at all.

*Opposite page: Delightful seventeenth-century pargeting, elaborately sculpted plaster door-case and a dated lintel on the Crown House in Newport, Essex.*

*Top left: A porch on a Georgian brick house in Beccles, Suffolk, made from wood and metal, with elaborate painted wrought-iron and delicate fretwork.*

*Above: A carved wooden porch in the Victorian Gothic Revival style in Gloucestershire.*

*Left: Elaborately sculpted and painted relief mouldings on a door in Clovelly, North Devon.*

**Canopies and hoods:** Sometimes these are flat, simple, moulded shelf-like projections above the door, perhaps displaying Classical influence in the brackets or consoles which support them. Other canopies rise in more elaborate shapes – arching, coved or carved. Baroque styles were current around 1700, and some of the soaring shell- or fan-like shapes prefigure the Georgian fanlight above the door. In the late nineteenth century a lace-like border of fretwork was often used to make a decorative finish.

A simpler and more homespun style of canopy is a single slope or a miniature gable, made like a mini-roof above the door (and preferably roofed with the same materials, whether tiles, slates or shingles). Some of the 'vernacular'-style porches of the turn of the century took inspiration from church lych gates.

To add a hood of this kind, take cues from the materials and architecture of the existing building, perhaps echoing the design of any barge-boards or the angle of the roof. If you intend to support it on wood or stucco brackets (these are only the visual means of support: it will also need to be structurally tied into the fabric of the wall), there may be some theme or motif on which you can commission a carving. The visible supports for a rustic version might be a pair of brackets in wrought iron rather than wood or stone.

**Decorative frames:** Some less polite and formal houses of the late eighteenth and early nineteenth centuries had filigree porches of wrought- or cast-iron work, creating a lacy frame around the door and contributing a rustic charm even to city houses, hinting

*Examples of simple and inexpensive door enhancement (from left):*

*White-painted wooden garden lattice and red-painted corrugated iron sheeting make a surprisingly elegant door surround on this Georgian brick house in Beccles, Suffolk.*

*An ornate but easily made wooden porch-type surround in England's West Country.*

*A simple canopy on the front door at Bathwick Hall in Bath, Avon, sensibly set beneath the fanlight so as not to diminish the amount of light it allows indoors.*

at honeysuckle and old-fashioned roses even when not used as plant supports. While there are modern replicas in cast iron, the prettifying effect can be achieved more simply with garden arches set around the doorway, especially if you can coax a curtain of annuals to clothe the mesh.

## WINDOWS: THE EYES OF THE HOUSE

It is tempting to call windows the eyes of a house. As with faces, some façades are good-looking, some commonplace, others full of character — and the eyes/windows make an important contribution to establishing a sense of personality. It is perhaps when there is something not quite right that the eyes analogy is most telling. It may be a matter of positioning or size, but more often it is a question of expression — a blank, mindless stare rather than the thoughtful gaze of a rational being, very often caused by the replacement of original windows with ones made of modern 'convenience' materials.

Sometimes the oddity is not derived from a change

to the window opening proper, but from some alteration in its periphery or something distracting that can be seen within. One misguided streamlining tactic is to remove ornamental mouldings above windows — like shaving off eyebrows. Occasionally the sin can be one of commission, such as the introduction of spurious shutters. Of course, there can equally be instances where such activities have the beneficial effect of a facelift. Scrutinize your house — perhaps with half-closed eyes — and see if any aspect of the windows strikes you as awkward or out of balance. Then consider whether this might be rectified by any cosmetic changes rather than anything as drastic as window transplants. Classical architects were so preoccupied with this question of balance that they often incorporated dummy windows into a façade to preserve the overall rhythm. These blanks might be delineated with the full set of pediments and mouldings to match the real windows, or be merely an outlined shape. Sometimes when a fake window was included in the wall its reveal was plastered and then it would be realistically painted with glazing bars and a blind. Another ruse was to paint *trompe l'oeil* mouldings in grisaille on the flat plastered wall around real or blank windows to create the effect of embellishments.

### New for old?

The problems of window replacement are not new. Windows are particularly vulnerable to weather as well as to fashion, and very old houses may have had several replacements in successive materials and styles. When, for instance, eighteenth-century houses were enlarged and extensively altered in the nineteenth century, many had their sash windows changed. The advent of mass-produced glass tempted many people to remove glazing bars and insert larger panes in the new style; other houses were fitted with new designs altogether, including bays. These changes offend purists since they transgress their canons of proportion and balance, but to many people who have become accustomed to the more eclectic and eccentric arrangements of Victorian and Arts and Crafts façades, some results can seem now pleasingly mellow, particularly when the replacements are themselves well made and graciously proportioned, and the building is harmonious overall.

The manner in which altering the windows can disrupt the established character of a building is particularly evident in a row or terrace. In houses built up to World War II the window detailing was often a

*A window in Tamerzet, Tunisia.*

carefully calculated pattern of balanced proportions and lines. Every aspect of a window counts: the shape of the opening, the shape and number of the panes and the position and moulding of glazing bars. There was sometimes a hidden logic in this organization: in the classically composed façades of the eighteenth century, for example, a precisely graded scale of proportions between windows on different storeys pertained. Those on the ground floor might be twice as high as their width, those on the first floor one and a third times the width, while those on the second or top floor were square. The harmonies were not always so elaborately articulated, but design effects were deliberately considered. Some pane layouts were organized to avoid a glazing bar cutting across the line of vision. Around the turn of the century large lower panes were topped with a pattern of smaller panes, partly for reasons to do with aesthetic balance and partly perhaps to help filter light: this arrangement is seen in both the Queen Anne subdivided sash above a plain one, and the small opening leaded light above a plain casement characteristic of early twentieth-century houses.

Whenever the original windows are replaced with ones in a different style or a different material, the intrinsic character of a building is diminished. Occasionally, as with the metal windows of Modernist 'Sun-trap' houses, original frames may have deteriorated beyond repair, but with many wooden sash and casement windows, repairs are feasible and less costly than replacement. Any draughts can be stopped by fitting unobtrusive pile brush strip into the gaps. If entire windows have to be replaced with copies, you can take the opportunity of having them made with unobtrusive double glazing, and getting hardwood draughtproofing strips incorporated in the joinery. Secondary glazing is another solution that does not interfere with the window's appearance.

One cause of the 'blank stare' of replacement windows in synthetic materials is their lack of depth: instead of having gracefully moulded frames and glazing bars, glass and surround form a single flat plane. Another of the charms of older sash windows and casements with leaded lights is the way the irregularities in the original crown glass create lively, rippling reflections.

*Top: Stone painted to look like brick on an English house in the West Country.*

*Right: Trompe l'oeil painted window surrounds in Granada, Spain.*

*Above: Rococo ornamentation on the stone walls around these simple windows on a house in Berchtesgaden in Bavaria, Germany.*

## Painting windows

White has become the acceptable colour for all sorts of windows. It teams well with every other colour and material and makes a good foil when a second main colour is used for, say, the front door. White is also an acceptable compromise when owners of houses forming a terrace want to impose a degree of uniformity. But brilliant white is a twentieth-century phenomenon. Previously windows were often painted cream, grey-white or a darker colour such as dark green, brown or black. Earlier in this century there was a vogue for painting windows in two colours: the outer frame might be brown or red and the inner, opening frame cream. The contemporary metal-frame windows, however, were painted brown, green or red – they were never painted white.

With more paint colours at our disposal than ever before, we can make windows part of a vigorous and exciting colour scheme, tying them in with doors, shutters, bargeboards and other woodwork. A good woodwork colour is also a positive way of unifying the disparate elements of a building with a chequered history of additions and alterations, in which varying styles of window often feature. By decisively painting all the woodwork green, say, you make it all 'belong'.

Painting is often extended to the window reveal, to lintels and sills and even to stucco surrounds on the façade. White or cream and stone-like colours are standard, but an alternative is to include this area in the woodwork scheme to give added emphasis.

# Shutters

Closed external shutters make a building look private, even forbidding, but their varying angles as they are opened and closed animate a façade. Shutters are most imposing when all are fastened open, doubling the size and thus the visual importance of the window openings. Such large expanses of woodwork offer exciting potential for a really positive colour scheme, especially if you like the extreme contrast of red or green shutters against white walls, or blue against yellowish stone. For a more restful effect take inspiration from the sunbleached palette of the Mediterranean and paint shutters in greys, pastels or low-intensity hues against pale walls.

As with doors, the construction of external shutters may be no more sophisticated than planks braced together, or it may be a good deal more refined, with handsome panelling that echoes woodwork elsewhere, and finely wrought hinges, handles and locks making a contribution like that of door fittings. Louvred shutters have a potential for looking good both on simple country buildings and on more formal houses. Shutters also offer a way of adding interest to a featureless modern façade, but beware of lightweight louvres, which can look effete, particularly if they are fixed open. They should have working hinges, and for an authentic touch the vents should slope outwards when they are closed, for rain to run off. More substantial board or panelled shutters might have more presence both open and closed.

*Left: A shuttered window in San Fidele near Siena in Italy.*

*Top right: Blue shutters with simple cut-out decoration on a stone house in Cornwall.*

*Middle: Shutters on Mykonos in the Greek islands.*

*Bottom: Blue shutters in Cornwall.*

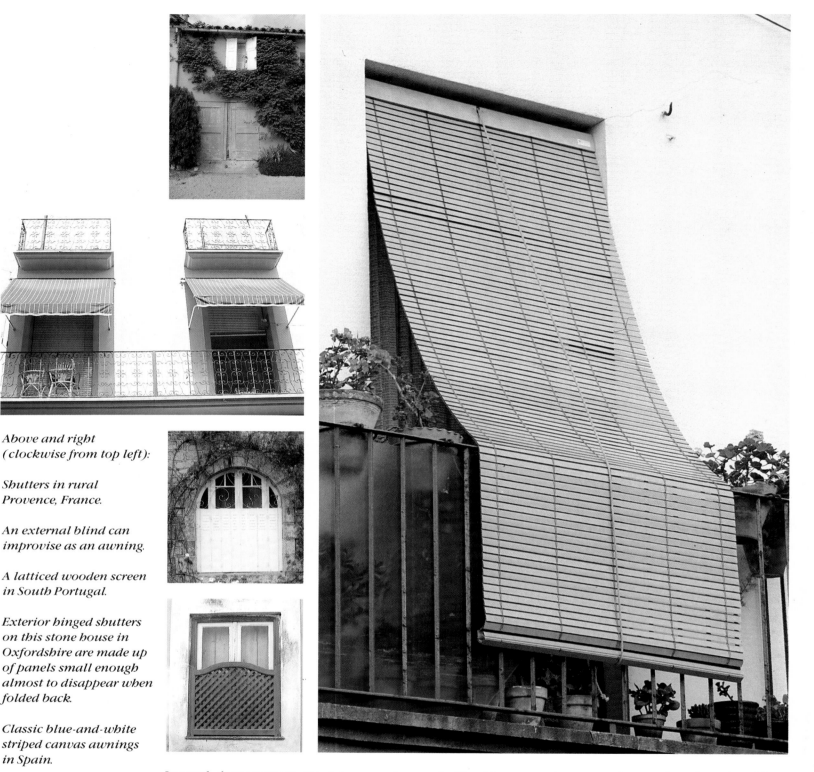

*Above and right
(clockwise from top left):*

*Shutters in rural
Provence, France.*

*An external blind can
improvise as an awning.*

*A latticed wooden screen
in South Portugal.*

*Exterior hinged shutters
on this stone house in
Oxfordshire are made up
of panels small enough
almost to disappear when
folded back.*

*Classic blue-and-white
striped canvas awnings
in Spain.*

Internal shutters were fitted to many houses built in the eighteenth and nineteenth centuries: they folded away neatly into the vertical casing at the sides of the window. Where they still exist (many have been removed and others are cemented fast by generations of paint) they should be treasured. Not only are they a precious original feature, but they deter intruders and keep out draughts. Unless they are of bare wood and you want them bare, you could treat them as a blank canvas and enhance with paint effects.

### Blinds, shades and awnings

A simple, unpretentious protection against sun is an exterior hanging blind made of natural rattan or slatted bamboo in dusky tones that rolls up with a cord.

More assertive are various styles of awning. Nineteenth-century houses sometimes still have the pelmet-like blind boxes at the top of their window reveals, and it would make an interesting project to discover the type of blind originally fitted and see if you can recreate it. Those with a roller mechanism project in a simple rectangle, while Dutch blinds, which have a hinged frame like a baby carriage hood, make a tighter, perkier shape. Early awnings were made of heavy canvas, often white striped with vermilion or green. You may like the eye-catching effect of stripes, or could choose an off-beat or sophisticated plain colour to complement or match the woodwork. Many different materials and styles are available from firms which provide blinds and awnings for shopfronts.

*Left: Interior shutters on a window of Chiddingstone Castle in Kent. This early manor house was extensively restored in the Gothick style during the eighteenth century.*

*Above: A Federal-style window and shutters in Georgetown, Washington D.C.*

## Inside the window

In daylight most windows reveal little of the interior other than a dark pool, so it is only in the immediate area of the window itself that any clues are given to what lies within. The fabric shapes of curtains and blinds are usually the only items indoors that transmit messages about the occupants to the outside world, but rarely is much thought given to the impression they make.

A façade with studied symmetry in its organization looks best when this is underpinned by equally similar window treatments. A repetition of the functional element – the roller blinds or plain sheers that filter out light and the gaze of the curious – unifies the windows from outside, and leaves you free to vary shapes and colours indoors. Windows can be treated as sets, too – those on the ground floor being treated one way, those upstairs another. When the windows themselves are an odd assortment, uniformity is less important, although some kind of repetition such as unity of colour or material is desirable. Whether your approach to windows is theatrical or understated, make sure that what shows on the outside is a generously proportioned, definite shape: avoid odd distracting angles or inscrutable pokes of fabric that look as if someone has forgotten to remove a dustsheet after a job.

You could try choosing an accent colour for curtains and blinds, perhaps matching that of the front door. For a more sophisticated effect the colour of

*Right: A typical eighteenth-century cordless sash window on a salt-box house in Lyme, Connecticut. The diagonal bar is to keep the window secure.*

*Below: Nothing looks nicer—from both outside and in—than a brightly coloured floral display in the window. The Scandinavians often paint vases of flowers on the exterior of window blinds.*

*Right: Red gingham and geraniums on a rural American summer cottage.*

*Far right: roller blinds which rise from the bottom offer the greatest of privacy with the maximum light and also look very elegant.*

the wall paintwork could be continued in the fabric at the windows: this would look dramatic in a mid-green, for instance, used in the same way through all the windows. The more assertive the colour, the more regular the windows need to be – and the fewer of them. If you choose an attention-seeking colour like yellow it will exaggerate any differences of shape or proportion.

Linings to curtains and blinds have traditionally been made in pale, neutral tones – a convenient colour that protected more ornate inner fabrics without itself being spoilt by fading. Nowadays, with fade-resistant sateen linings available in bright, rich colours, if you choose neutrals it has to be for a positive reason. Light-coloured linings remain the best choice for pale or translucent fabrics where any stronger colour would interfere with the cool theme; and light or intense colours 'read' best from outside – the subtlety of murky shades will tend to be lost behind the glass. Fabrics chosen for their colour message should be hung in the form of blinds or linings, right against the window.

## PLANTS: GROWING ARCHITECTURE

Interior designers use houseplants and flowers to put the final touches to their compositions, finding that they bring rooms to life in a way that no other element can. The same rule applies outside the house. Plants in key positions on the façade are somehow more than merely decorative: they add a dimension to the inanimate materials of the building.

Plants on the outside of the house should be treated with the same rigour and discrimination as are applied to flower arrangements indoors. Choose colours and textures, for example, for their positive contribution to the overall scheme. Make sure the style and material of containers flatter both the background of the building and the plants growing in them. Compose plant elements as deliberately as you compose the ornaments on a shelf or mantelpiece.

Plants may be seen as growing architectural elements related to the appearance of the whole building, and should be positioned for emphasis, following architectural cues – a trough placed squarely beneath

*Pelargoniums cascading from a windowsill in the ancient Italian capital, Rome.*

*Massed hanging
baskets in Mayfield,
East Sussex.*

a window, for example. Reinforce the regularity of a formal façade with symmetrically positioned shrubs or window-boxes. Where the features of a building are not regular, plants can be deployed to improve matters or disguise oddities. A climber or plants in a substantial container can be grown to act as a counter-weight in an asymmetrical façade, creating the necessary balance. Suspending a window-box beneath the sill will deepen the rectangular shape of a shallow window. Wall plants can visually anchor the building like buttresses. Climbers can clothe and curtain a bare or ugly surface. Plants can of course be purely decorative, too – a hanging basket or a plant pot adds the finishing touch to a façade in the same way that a carved finial or an ornamental keystone might. And they also have powerful distraction value: a stunning

plant display can draw attention from duller corners.

Plants whose role is to provide decorative detailing on the building itself (as opposed to being part of the garden proper – a subject of the next chapter) fall into three groups. There are 'shelf' plants that line up (or seem to) along windowsills and over door canopies, in the horizontal plane. There are plants in hanging baskets and decorative brackets, suspended like lamps to brighten a specific area. And thirdly, there are plants that grow vertically up the walls or use walls for support.

In all of these options flowers and flower colours can play a major or minor role against a furnishing of foliage. The choice is so extensive that it is possible to find plants to suit every aspect and situation and every exterior colour scheme.

*Above (clockwise from top left):*

*A hanging basket teeming with pelargoniums, lobelia, impatiens, petunias and helichrysums against a timber wall.*

*A characteristically studied arrangement against a Chinese window.*

*Pelargoniums tumbling from wall-mounted boxes.*

*Lobelia, pelargoniums and petunias against a black-and-white-painted Gothick cottage window.*

## Window-boxes

According to your type of window, a window-box may rest on the sill or be fixed on brackets on the wall below it. Make sure not only that you have fixings – and walls – that can take the weight, but that no planning restrictions prohibit this kind of decoration on your street.

Choose a material that harmonizes with those of the house – terracotta where there are reddish bricks, for instance. Choose a style in keeping with the spirit of the building – formal, ornate, rustic – or stick to the simplest shapes. Hardwood containers can be left in their natural state (protected with suitable preservative), while softwood window-boxes should be painted, preferably to match the woodwork of the window, and this colour then becomes a foil for the flower and leaf colours you choose. Many Classical designs are reproduced in both reconstituted stone and fibreglass: choose the latter where weight might be a problem. Try to avoid plastic, except for inner pots sunk out of view in the trough: keeping the flowering element in square pots (which butt together closely) allows a quick change between seasons.

A cheerful muddle of colours in cottage-garden style or the patriotic combination of red, white and blue can be disarmingly pretty in unselfconscious situations. Single-colour planting or a carefully orchestrated scheme based on a restricted palette makes the most powerful and potentially sophisticated impact, however. You can draw on the wide repertoire of named cultivars to get just the designer shade of petunia or pansy to match or tone with your other key colours. It is possible to keep an evergreen furnishing of, say, ivy and to replace the flowers (per-

haps, but not necessarily, changing to a different colour theme) each season. Just as you choose colour for your window frames and barge-boards, you are painting with flowers, and aiming for an effect that looks interesting but also 'right'. Incidentally, window-box displays are visible from indoors, too, so before you plant a jazzy display of African marigolds, make sure the scheme inside the room can take it.

## Hanging baskets

Composing a shapely hanging basket is more like flower arranging than most other planting activities: you can take full advantage of the trailing and creeping habits of plants to make an attractive display in the round. Whether colours are mixed or co-ordinated has an influence on style, as in window-box planting. One under-exploited colour scheme for a mid-toned background concentrates on flowers in yellows and whites, perhaps with the pale grey, lime green or variegated foliage of *Helichrysum petiolare* instead of the usual greenery. Against a white or pale background, stronger colours are more telling.

One hanging basket can be pleasing, but the effect is strengthened by repetition. A pair, symmetrically placed, adds emphasis. A series of similarly planted baskets equally spaced along the front of a building sets up a striking design rhythm.

Whether free-standing baskets are suspended overhead or half-round baskets are attached to walls, fixings must be secure. Access for watering is vital, since hanging baskets should never be allowed to dry out. Indeed, watering more than once a day may be necessary, so think again if you are not able to fulfil this requirement.

*Lush bougainvillaea forms a stunning frame for this wrought-iron-clad window.*

## Growing upwards

Some plants climb naturally by means of tendrils or clinging pads; others must be tied and trained in place. There is a vast choice in terms of colour, foliage texture, flowering season, soil and aspect suitability and so on, but one of the main 'architectural' considerations is the general habit of the plant: whether it twines and sprawls in exuberant natural garlands, or is well-behaved, amenable to clipping and shaping, and therefore suitable for controlled use, like a building block of foliage.

The first category tends towards the romantic look, and wisteria, roses, clematis and honeysuckle can all create interest on a plain terraced house, keeping faith with the cottage spirit that imbues many styles of architecture, particularly where there is some ironwork or a porch to support it. This effect is stunning during the more or less ephemeral flower season, when carefully chosen colours can transform the whole façade. Some flowers offer the bonus of scent, too. Out of season, though, in the leafless winter months, the tangle of stems is hard to keep well groomed, and so is more acceptable on an informal,

or mellowed-by-time, sort of house rather than on austere, prim and proper façades.

Another design option is to allow a leafy covering – preferably evergreen for all-year-round effect – to clothe the wall. The plants that would fulfil this function are self-clinging ones like true ivy (species of *Hedera*), or the deciduous Virginia creeper and Boston ivy. The more vigorous species of these incline towards total cover-up, with attendant structural threat, but you can choose a more compact cultivar: variegated-leaf ivies, for example, are generally slower-growing than their all-green cousins. Or you can train them rather strictly. Dense green leaves have the potential for making geometric shapes, and you could use ivy rather like topiary work in a single plane, to enhance symmetry. Alternatively, they can be used like weatherboard or tiling, as cladding, up to the line of a string course. A striking way of creating visual depth along one boundary in a small courtyard is to train ivy to frame 'archways' of flat wall, and this simple foliage effect could be adapted for the blank side wall of a house; many ivies can and do tolerate a shady situation.

*Above: Greenery can also sometimes perform the function of shutters, screening the windows from excess light or ensuring privacy, as here at Sizergh Castle in the English Lake District. The castle has been the home of the Strickland family since 1239.*

*Left: Sculpting the growth of greenery around a window or door can produce spectacular decorative effects, as here again at Sizergh Castle's fourteenth-century Pele Tower.*

In a favourable climate the cover-up can be a colourful one such as bougainvillea, whose vibrant tones ranging through the reds from distinctly bluish to warmly coppery orange mean that any paint colour in the vicinity needs careful vetting to prevent clashes. Another course of action is to grow colourful annuals against the wall – ipomoea, sweet peas, nasturtiums, eccremocarpus – either for colour on their own, or to brighten a host evergreen.

Candidates for the 'buttress' principle are dense foliage plants (not climbers) that can be grown against a wall, trained to shape and further clipped and tailored. Box, yew, privet and bay are famous for their potential as topiary subjects. Shrubs like berberis, pyracantha, *Euonymus fortunei* and cherry laurel can also be moulded to wall-hugging shapes, while herringbone cotoneaster stretches its flat branches in a more informal arch. Some of these plants light up a colour scheme with flowers or fruit in season. On a house with appropriate paintwork, the powdery blue flowers of a ceanothus, for example, would look very striking.

Providing supports for climbing plants helps keep them under control. An unobtrusive grid can be made by securing galvanized wire to vine eyes fixed in the wall. A more conspicuous and decorative support system may be made by attaching a panel of trellis against the wall. It is possible to rig up both these devices so that they can be unhooked and gently lowered to the ground with the plants attached when the wall needs repainting or repointing. Beware, on older and fragile walls, of vigorous plants such as ivy, wisteria, Russian vine and Virginia creeper, which can not only damage soft bricks and friable mortar, but choke gutters and invade roof spaces.

Some climbers and wall shrubs will grow in containers set against the base of the wall, but others can be planted in prepared pockets of soil about 50cm/2ft square at the base of the wall. (The roots can often spread and find nourishment beneath an adjacent path, but beware of vigorous root-runs that invade drains and disrupt footings.) Check the aspect and soil requirements of each plant: mortar in the wall can make soil conditions at its base somewhat alkaline, so a lime-hater like ceanothus would need to have the soil adjusted.

## EXTERIOR LIGHTING

Before looking at light fittings in any detail, the various purposes that you would like your outside lighting to serve should be considered. You may wish to have a beacon to summon the traveller or a searchlight to betray an intruder; a light to find your keys by; a means of identifying a visitor before you open the door; safe access via steps and paths; a highlight for the name or number of your house; a way of displaying some attractive feature of the house or the immediate garden; and a way of welcoming visitors.

### Seeing the light

The enormous range of light fittings available can make choice difficult. The emphasis in many brochures and showrooms is on period-look replicas of traditional models (which are virtually all anachronistic), but other ranges carry more straightforward designs, from lamps with clean modern lines to those reflecting aspects of industrial high-tech. Most of these fittings are chosen for their looks, and while many of them may indeed provide efficient illumination of the sort you want as well as a message about your style, they may go only part of the way towards fulfilling the various lighting needs of your exterior, and need to be supplemented by other kinds of lighting.

The front door is usually the focal point of the façade, and most exterior lighting is used to enhance it. The lamp conventionally positioned beside the door offers a signal of welcome, its decorative aspects adding a personal touch, but it is often more important for its symbolic value than for its efficiency as a light source.

One course of action is to dispense with visible

light fittings altogether and use light sources where the fittings themselves are not on display, such as spotlights and wall-washing floodlights. You might associate these types of lighting with theatrical *son et lumière* effects and think them inappropriate on the domestic front, but they can be surprisingly effective. A well-positioned directional light, highlighting some architectural feature such as a door surround, will reflect enough illumination to make doorstep transactions efficient. While interior lighting depends a good deal on reflected light, which bounces off the pale surfaces of walls and ceilings, outdoors this effect is minimal, although more light will bounce off a light-coloured wall, particularly a smooth painted stucco, for example, than off matt brick or stone. Front doorway surrounds are often finished in a comparatively reflective surface which makes them stand out more clearly and also fits them more for

*Top left: Standing lights set amidst foliage provide good illumination and produce an attractive effect.*

*Left: Downlighting or wallwashers are spectacular and very effective for the lighting of the exteriors of buildings.*

*Hidden spotlights or uplighters trained to illuminate trees, shrubs or foliage can produce very effective 'night gardens'. Coloured lights, used judiciously, can also produce spectacular effects.*

this kind of lighting treatment.

Neat light fittings built into steps are a splendid way of lighting a potentially tricky area without entering the realms of decorative display. Low, downward-directed pedestal lights along a path can also be unobtrusive and neutral in design. Both of these measures may be used to complement more ornamental lighting effects around the door.

Doorways incorporating glazing can be dramatically lit at night, particularly those with decorative fanlights, which reveal their tracery, and panels of stained or etched glass, which come into their own for the benefit of the outside world and not just for the pleasure of the occupants, as during daylight. The amount of useful light from these sources as a side effect of their decorative value varies with the design, but if you need to supplement it, try not to choose any method that will diminish their dramatic effect. A

display light fitting could both clash in style with and dilute the glow of the main feature. A wash of light from a hidden source or neat functional lamps fitted in the steps might be more suitable.

Sometimes a doorway is too grand or too oddly composed to allow for a conspicuous decorative fitting. For example, you would want to avoid choosing anything to clash in style or prominence with a Classical Coade stone keystone or an elaborate pediment; some off-centre doorways in Arts and Crafts style are too intricately designed to take an added complication; and sometimes there is simply nowhere to put a light fitting. The answer may be to use indirect lighting from a source at ground level such as a spot (make sure the beam doesn't dazzle people at the door) or wall-washing floodlight. A recessed doorway or porch could in this way have its inner surfaces bathed in inviting light.

*Right (clockwise from top left):*

*A useful garden light which is impervious to bad weather and spreads its light downwards to illuminate the ground and thus does not produce glare at eye level.*

*A large ornamental outdoor lantern on a stone house in Germany.*

*A traditional early nineteenth-century corner-mounted lantern on the wall of an old rectory in Norfolk.*

*A candle lantern complete with reflector, now wired for electric light on a wall in Essex, Connecticut.*

*Top left: Greenery around wall lighting can be striking.*

*Top right (clockwise):*

*Hanging lights are very effective in small yards.*

*A lantern in Charleston, South Carolina.*

*A cast-iron carriage lamp.*

## Appropriate fittings

Houses in a Classical vein can take formal treatment — perhaps even the obligatory pair of carriage lamps. The better the house the grander should be the lamps, and the more chance you have of being able to pinpoint a period look that is appropriate. There are dozens of handsome reproductions, and the occasional antique may be available from an architectural salvage company. It takes formal symmetry to justify a matching pair of lamps, one on either side of the door or atop pillars at the base of a flight of steps. If your house is not symmetrical, but substantial enough to merit more than one fitting in one of the traditional styles, you could balance a single wall-mounted lamp near the door with a second post- or pillar-mounted one of the same design nearby.

As with door fittings, both brass and iron with a black finish are 'traditional' materials. Only the grandest and most elegant homes would have opted for brass in the past, and it is easy to overdo the grandeur and look ridiculous. Choose brass if the rest of the façade lives up to it, otherwise opt for the lower-key texture of black. Decoration etched or cut in the glass of the lamps should also be chosen only if the façade is imposing enough.

For traditional-style country cottages or plain terraced houses, simple lanterns look in keeping. Also effective on not-too-prettified artisan cottages are bulkhead lights: their functional appearance is in tune with the plain workaday style of ledged and braced doors and simple porch hoods.

## Practical notes

Modern replicas and designs have the advantage of being made in weatherproof materials and finishes, which remain functional at very low temperatures. They can be wired for long-lasting low-energy lamps, which are ideal since outside lighting tends to be left on for prolonged periods. You can even buy a special bulb that simulates the soft glow of gas lighting, to complete the authentic effect of a reproduction gas lamp-post.

Time switches are valuable for outside lighting, and so are detector devices which switch lights on when people or vehicles move in a monitored area. These are useful both as a deterrent to burglars and as a welcome to homecomers.

Another way of welcoming guests by means of lighting is with temporary party-night strategies: lining the garden path with flares, edging the steps with low-voltage flexible cable studded with lamps, stringing miniature fairy lights in the trees and around the doorway, and decking the house front with lanterns.

# THE LARGER VIEW

Beyond the actual four walls of every exterior there usually lies a stretch of territory which is closely visually linked with it, be it the landscaped garden of a large house or merely the tiny area where you and your neighbours store the garbage! Any such area can be made to work towards exterior enhancement in countless imaginative ways.

*Left: A balcony on an eighteenth-century house in Sicily.*
*Above: Detail of a decorative Victorian porch in Surrey.*

*Right: In a warm gregarious country, like Italy, balconies become lively centres of activity. Here, in Verona, beautiful eighteenth-century murals make a splendid backdrop to this open-air living space.*

*Below right: Balconies are a popular means by which modern architects give extra space, interest and ornament to their buildings.*

People have always been tempted to take a feature intended for some practical purpose and turn it into something ornamental. The exterior of buildings may be 'function into art' on rather a grand scale, but is no less subject to the urge to adorn and decorate. How dull so many houses would look without their pretty porches and porticoes; and why slap down a plain concrete path from here to there when it can describe delightful herringbone patterns in brick or stone as it curves seductively into the distance?

## EXTENDING THE EXTERIOR

There are several ways in which we traditionally like to extend our homes, including balconies, conservatories, porches and patios. These additions provide increased comfort and convenience, stretching precious living space a little further and creating a kind of hybrid area combining indoors and out. These are hard-working and difficult features to design and plan successfully: they must never look 'tacked-on' and inappropriate, or spoil the charm and dignity of the original building through thoughtless choice of scale and style. While such additions need to look good, they must also remain wholly practical in use both from within and from the street or the garden outside the house. Satisfying this dual role successfully is pos-

sible, however, and looking at examples of such features that have been incorporated by the architect of similar houses in construction will show you what can be done. Historical traditions have also played a part in determining the style and position of a particular extension.

The initial practical need for an exterior addition has often encouraged a distinctive regional style that is quickly and easily identified. Those regimented rows of small curly ironwork balconies are immediately reminiscent of Spain or Italy where they provide a welcome place to sit, and a breath of fresh air to

*This page, far left bottom: A post-modern balcony with simple but effective decoration, including a leaded central window which incorporates a stained glass panel.*

*Near left (clockwise from top):*

*A bold modern statement made by a prow-like balcony on the Wachter Villa in Antwerp, Belgium.*

*Aggressively modern balcony design on an Israeli apartment building still gives scope for more traditional personal ornament.*

*Tiered verandah and balconies can be the main statement of an exterior. Here on this German house, minimal colour use allows Nature to provide the accent.*

*A Regency balcony in London's Hampstead.*

interior rooms during hot dusty summer months. Sultry weather is also the incentive for the traditional colonial-style verandah or back porch, ubiquitous in Australia and America, a charming architectural feature originally developed to shade the interior from the fading and debilitating effects of strong sunshine and making a delightfully cool place to relax. At the other end of the scale, the storm porch is a familiar and necessary refuge for owners of rustic cottages and cabins subjected to strong gales or blizzards. On an elegant town house where perhaps privacy and prestige are more highly valued, the porch represents a status symbol and creates a useful reception area which also serves to distance the home a little further from the hustle and bustle of the street outside.

Whatever the purpose and location of all these features, their appearance has become so essential to the overall look of a property that it is easy to take their practical role for granted. We concentrate on using them to amuse, to add balance or to focus attention; we decorate them, extend them, even pick them out in bright colours to add emphasis; or smother them in plants to encourage them to blend with the main fabric of the building.

*Fine carved wooden
balconies on the 1899
Asendorf House, in
Savannah, Georgia.*

## Balconies

The balcony is perhaps the element least likely to be added to an existing building. Visually it enhances the windows or the façade of a building and has usually been planned and designed by the original architect. A small wrought-iron balcony little bigger than a hay-rack may simply extend from the window area, or a much larger one constructed in timber and concrete might cover the full width of the wall. On some buildings it may be little more than an ornamental stone parapet on top of a large bay window; or in the case of flats or apartments, a single large balcony may be divided by some form of partitioning into separate units. Some larger types may even be accessible via a separate staircase extending into the street or garden.

The balcony itself can be plain or fancy: in metal, timber or concrete, depending on the style and location of the house or apartment block. Some of the wrought ironwork seen in Sydney, New Orleans and Seville is outstanding in its curly decorative detail, while many traditional timber buildings in the Austrian Tyrol, Newport, Rhode Island, and in English medieval market towns are often embellished with the most beautiful carvings and cut-outs. A balcony serves a dual purpose: it is a support for plants to decorate the outside of the building as well as a modest but often delightful high-rise patio area.

For safety in use, this elegantly suspended feature

*Far left: On this turn-of-the-century Australian house, wooden balcony railings are intricately filigreed.*

*Left top: A restrained balcony on an early Georgian house, in London's Richmond.*

*Left bottom: The characteristic cast-iron balconies of the French Quarter of New Orleans are an essential part of the city's great charm.*

must be structurally sound and given adequate support in order to be able to take a person's weight, otherwise it should be treated as purely ornamental. Plants and pots can also be heavy, particularly when filled with damp soil. To reduce their weight, use light fibreglass pots which come in a wide range of shapes and styles imitating heavier, natural materials such as clay and stone; and select a lightweight peatless compost mixture, the kind which uses beads of perlite or vermiculite to add bulk and good drainage. Keeping the weight down may make containers unstable where plants are tall or bulky; stabilize them by fixing them with metal ties securely to the floor or side supports of the balcony. Hardy plants – those that can withstand a certain amount of exposure to strong sunshine and keen winds – should be chosen for balconies. These should include trailing and creeping species which can be encouraged to spill over the front and down the wall. All plants in containers need frequent watering and should be stood in troughs or saucers to catch excess moisture; if water for such plants is allowed to spill out and down the wall this could not only cause a nuisance to passers-by but might also eventually lead to damage of the structure of the building.

A balcony may open off any rooms, even a bathroom, and can provide a wonderful extension for any of them. It is not just the impression of leafiness beyond the French windows that gives pleasure: a collection of culinary herbs outside the kitchen would be really useful in a high-rise apartment with no garden; and a display of exotic ferns on a sheltered balcony will give the impression of a lush jungle view from a bathroom or sitting room. If there is room for chairs and a table, informal alfresco meals may be enjoyed in fine weather. If the balcony is to be used for sitting out, it should be provided with some kind of screening and shelter – not just for privacy, but also as protection from wind and rain as, like roof gardens, balconies tend to be rather exposed. Side-screens may be erected in any lightweight material depending on the effect you are hoping to create: timber, bamboo, metal mesh or clear plastic. It may also be a good idea to plan some form of overhead protection from strong sunshine or light showers. This might take the shape of a timber pergola threaded with a flowering climber such as honeysuckle or exotic passion flower (*Passiflora*); or a brightly coloured retractable fabric or plastic awning. These can be carefully chosen for colour and style, to co-ordinate with paint colour on door and window frames or to make a lovely splash of brightness on an otherwise dull façade. They are a common sight in sunny cities like San Francisco and throughout the Mediterranean, where their stripes and primary colours are a cheery sight in the strong light.

*Above: Cronkhill in Shropshire, built by John Nash in 1803, was the first Italianate villa to be built in Britain and makes a strong feature of its verandahs and porches.*

*Right: A carved wooden porch dating from around 1870 in Mystic, Connecticut.*

## Verandahs

On ground level, a verandah serves a similar purpose to a balcony – it offers a pleasant shady place to sit and protection from strong sunshine for the rooms within – but with the advantage of shelter from wind and rain too. Again styles vary, but generally the structure is slightly raised and made of brick, stone or timber. It can be extended around one, two, three or all four sides of a building depending on prevailing weather conditions and how good the views are; and being long and narrow, space is normally restricted to a few pieces of furniture: seating, perhaps a table; a limited selection of plants in containers and possibly the occasional Classical statue to emphasize elegant

*This cool and enclosed Australian verandah exemplifies the spirit of blending the inside and the outdoors.*

*Above: The verandah often doubles as a grandly inviting entrance, as here on the Asendorf House in Savannah, Georgia.*

*Left: The open and spare porch on a Stick-style house, dating from around 1870, in Glastonbury, Connecticut.*

stone surroundings. The verandah may be open at the front and sides, for use only in the warmer months; enclosed to waist level; or even partly glazed to provide extra shelter. It is frequently highly decorative with elegant pilasters and columns or with striking mouldings, carvings and cornice details. The verandah is usually sheltered enough to be able to use upholstered furniture, seasonally at least: cushions slung on wooden or brass poles along the back wall make an excellent backrest for bench seating where restricted space does not allow the use of free-standing garden furniture.

For a similar effect but avoiding major construction work, you can always erect a pergola made of timber,

trellis or brick or a combination of these materials, with low wooden decking underfoot to create a clean, level surface for seating and plants. Strongly fastened to the house wall and smothered in an attractive evergreen or summer-flowering climber, this arrangement will provide shade and shelter as well as an attractive feature on the outside of the building.

The verandah is not intended primarily to display plants – it is more a place for relaxing and enjoying the view without being prey to the elements. Because it is deliberately shady, plants are usually restricted to formal arrangements of evergreen shrubs, climbers and sometimes small trees in tubs and containers, which can be moved outside during summer.

*Top: A very straightforward 'lean-to' conservatory.*

*Above: The conservatory on Mark Twain's House in Hartford, Connecticut, built in the Stick style between 1874 and 1881.*

*Left: The galleried octagonal conservatory on Tyninghame Castle, near Scotland's capital, Edinburgh. This modern addition was designed to blend harmoniously with the 1829 building.*

## Conservatories

For those looking for a jungle effect or who have a passion for plants, a conservatory or sunroom is the ideal, providing a controllable environment for more tender species and a weatherproof place in which to enjoy them. These stylish, mostly glass, extensions can be a real asset both visually, as a decorative feature, and as a useful extra indoor living area with a special kind of atmosphere. The structure may be an elegant survivor from the last century: an old hothouse for collectable exotics; an orangery spanning the back of the house; or a once leafy indoor/outdoor sitting room reminiscent of a more leisurely age. Many of these wonderful old buildings have crumbled from neglect and more often the conservatory is a recent addition. Yet the old styles are as popular as they ever were and the majority of newly built conservatories are virtually indistinguishable from the originals on which they are based: using modern, easier-to-maintain materials but copying every detail down to the carvings and mouldings. The old-fashioned styles can look as good on a newer property as they do on a traditional one, provided that they are positioned carefully. A wide range of styles in an extensive choice of sizes, shapes and designs can be purchased as component parts to be assembled on site. Alternatively, where the location is awkward or something a little more unusual is required, custom-made or architect-designed conservatories are frequently erected in both traditional and ultra-modern solar styles. New architect-designed homes may often incorporate a conservatory-type area to catch maximum sunlight – the whole principle of the

conservatory perfectly in step with modern thinking on the use of glass and solar power.

The inherent charm and flexibility of conservatories mean that they can be positioned virtually anywhere to great visual effect: not just at ground level, but on top of a flat-roofed single-storey extension; in an awkward corner; tucked into a side passage; and even on a roof, if it is strong enough to take the weight of the structure. You might sometimes see a two-storey conservatory, offering sun-room facilities to two rooms in the house, or making a superb feature of a high, fully glazed roof. A long, narrow conservatory packed with plants is also an excellent way to link two parts of a building together or to join the main house to a much-used outbuilding such as a storeroom, workshop or pool house. Where there is no room for one, taking out the roof of a single-storey room and replacing it with an ornamental glass one may sometimes be done to produce a light, airy conservatory atmosphere.

The main structure can be timber – painted white or stained – or metal finished in white, silver or bronze, and it usually has a brick, stone-faced or timber base to match the house construction. Design can embrace a wide variety of architectural styles from arches and curves to Gothic sweeps and pinnacles, with mouldings, crests and all kinds of embellishment added to order. The conservatory can look as pretty and ornate as an iced wedding cake or as smart and sleek as a crystal pyramid or glassy igloo, depending on preferred style. Whatever style is chosen, it rarely looks ugly or out of place, since the structure is almost exclusively glass, which reflects nearby buildings, trees and plants and also bounces back any available light, and so it is wonderful at blending chameleon-like into its surroundings. Like a porch or lean-to, it is also a marvellous insulator, making rooms within instantly warmer; and it creates the perfect transition between house and garden, especially if filled with plants and fitted with double doors that can be left open in fine weather.

Conservatories are used in a great many ways. Traditionally they were plant houses: hot and humid to support a jungle of tender species, with perhaps a cast-iron or hardwood table and bench or chairs for perusing the latest seed catalogues or reading the paper. Today they are often more comfortable, and might be centrally heated and double glazed, used as a kitchen extension, extra sitting room or even a first-floor bathroom, to make the most of that wonderful light and solar warmth. They make excellent housing for swimming pools too.

They are not, however, easy to decorate. The large expanse of glass needs screening when the sun is at its hottest, and the most efficient method employs external slatted screens which, while producing fabulous striped shadows inside, are not particularly attractive when viewed from outside. The alternative is internal blinds in rattan, timber or plastic, often with automatic light-sensitive controls to prevent the temperature rising too high. Good automatic ventilation is equally important, but the addition of heating, double glazing and humidification control depends on how the room is being used.

*Right (clockwise from top left):*

*An typical English suburban porch, built like a tiny conservatory.*

*An early nineteenth-century stone porch in the Gothic Revival manner in Painswick, Gloucestershire.*

*A late eighteenth-century Federal-style porch on Chestnut Street in Salem, Massachusetts.*

*Neighbouring Victorian cottages in Oxford share a carved wooden porch.*

*Another Federal-style porch on Salem's Chestnut Street, this one dating from the early nineteenth century.*

*A simply made Post-modern porch.*

*A typical street entrance in Charleston, South Carolina, where a deceptively convicing 'front door' is actually a gate leading to the verandah.*

## Porches

A small conservatory might make a good and rather attractive enclosed porch area, particularly a style with a central ridge and the appropriate decorative details. More often, though, porches are built of stone, brick or timber to match the style of the house, with glazing restricted to fixed windows and sometimes a door. Whether it is completely enclosed, open on all sides or partly walled or glazed at the sides, depends on how it is used and how ornamental it is intended to look. Where space is restricted or where a large, enclosed structure might look out of proportion, the porch might only comprise a small roof or canopy over the front door. A more decorative pitched roof may be supported by stone columns, trelliswork or

brick. On a town house, a painted entablature (a decorative frame with ornamental canopy effect over the door) helps dress up the front door a little. A more elaborate enclosed construction in town or country may have room for bench seating, shelves of plants and umbrella stands. In the suburbs it has become popular to glass in the porch area or to add a brand new, mainly glass, porch to provide a little weatherproofing and somewhere to grow plants.

In many cases, though, an ornamental hood or porch will already exist as an integral part of the architecture of a building. Sometimes, on a terraced row of cottages or town houses, in apartment entrances or semi-detached dwellings, there may be shared or double porches, either back to back for

*The delightfully elaborate porch on Pingtree House in Salem, Massachusetts.*

privacy or more friendly pairs of front doors sharing the same canopy.

Porches are sometimes used to create a grand entrance, a stunning focal point designed to impress, even intimidate. Others simply say welcome, especially at night when clever lighting can be used to enhance their effect. Occasionally a porch may be extended into a covered walkway, making the approach to the house very grand indeed. This walkway might be as elaborate as a glassed-in conservatory-like structure linking front door to gate, or a simple timber- or brick-supported roof offering a little shade and shelter.

Otherwise, modern double-glazed glass boxes apart, the porch seems to provide home owners with

a wonderful opportunity to display their individuality with all kinds of idiosyncratic styles and ingenious ideas. Whatever their period and location, they are often decorated with intricate lattice work, carvings, trimmings, scrolls and cut-outs, and with wrought iron, stucco or painted terracotta rosettes. And even modest types might be flanked by statuary, potted plants or lamps.

It is one of the pleasures of looking at house exteriors, in town and country, to spot unusual porch styles and treatments. Do it regularly with an attentive eye and you will see a pattern closely linked to location and use. Town porches frequently go for grandeur, with Classic columns and pillars, pediments, stained-glass or ornamental fanlights, and a pair of smart

*Left: This neo-classical porch is, surprisingly, in Rio de Janeiro, Brazil.*

*Above (clockwise from top):*

*A stained-glass porch in Bradford, West Yorkshire.*

*A classic modern porch.*

*An 1870s porch in Mystic, Connecticut.*

*A view through columned porches in London's Bayswater.*

shrubs or trees in matching tubs or pots on either side of the steps or doorway. In coastal areas you will see home-made and imaginative porches, their exterior stripped by keen salt-laden winds and used to store fishing rods, windbreaks and spades, and displaying a miscellany of beachcomber 'finds' such as driftwood, seaweed, shells and other flotsam washed up and retrieved. It is in the country that the porch works hardest for its living: home to muddy boots and coats, it must stand firm against the worst gales and winter weather. Usually built of stout timber or solid stone, it is often given its character by the roof, which tends to take its style from the main roof of the house: thatched, tiled or slated, to produce a visually satisfying link in miniature. With thatched cottages, a scaled-down arrangement of thatch over the front door is often porch enough. Bigger porches are the natural place to store boots, baskets, bags and other useful

tackle and family paraphernalia.

Roses and honeysuckle round the door are of course obligatory for the picturesque country cottage, and a simple support smothered in a mass of foliage and flowers may serve as a perfectly pretty 'porch'. But evergreen ivies, Virginia creeper with its splendid late-season colour and other vigorous climbers are equally decorative. Nor are they restricted to rural residences: you may as easily see the town-house porch beautifully disguised beneath the scented pendulous blooms of wisteria, a climbing hydrangea or lovely passion flower.

## PAVING THE WAY

No building can be viewed or appreciated out of context. However beautifully designed, built and maintained, its immediate surroundings can make or mar the effect. Even a broken-down fence or pile of uncleared rubble or rubbish can be enough to create a sense of neglect, while the wrong kind of feature – perhaps constructed to an inappropriate scale or in a mismatching style – can look uncomfortably incongruous, even disastrous to the dignity and appearance of the property. It might only be a small detail such as an undersized window-box or hanging basket totally lost against a grand façade, or perhaps a complete backyard patio or front-garden scheme in which, for example, Classical statues and smart city paving make an old country cottage look rumpled and shabby; or a modest ornamental fountain and pool can be completely outclassed by a superb country manor house or imposing town villa. Even the choice of plant containers can have a significant effect on the total look and the right period style: choosing rustic terracotta or elegant Versailles tubs as appropriate can enhance a stylish patio or front step.

The area immediately around a house needs decorating with especial care. It stimulates that vital initial impression on the approach to the building, and is also the first thing seen when looking out from inside, and so it is desirable that reactions to it are immediate and positive. It helps to have some kind of style theme, prompted by the type and size of property, so that the various elements hang together well and look good. Building materials such as brick or stone can be matched to the main fabric of the building and even echoed in random features around the garden to pull the scheme together. With an older property, this may mean searching salvage yards for second-hand bricks and timbers to achieve the correct weathered appearance and the impression that a feature has been there for years. The rawness of new materials is always obvious, although there are ways of softening and prematurely ageing them: by rubbing with dung, yoghurt and other old recommended remedies; or, more pleasantly perhaps, by encouraging mosses, ivies and other vigorous climbers and creepers to grow. Choice of plants can also significantly affect the total look: certain species automatically create a strong rustic atmosphere, while others suggest an Oriental scheme or stately elegance.

Equally important, this area forms the link between indoors and out, and should ideally blend naturally both with the rooms within and the garden, yard or

*Right: A modern ornamental cast-iron balcony and trellis frame make the most of this patio garden and are in perfect harmony with the Victorian house and its detail.*

*Far right: A wooden trellis frame creates a verandah effect in this pretty patio garden.*

street. It is usual to have a paved area or at least some firm, dry surface immediately beyond outer doors and French windows to keep feet clean and to provide firm standing for plant containers, furniture and the other trappings of 'outdoor living'. This is where the boundaries between house and garden become blurred, especially in regions enjoying a hot climate and where the terrace or loggia is a much-used extension of the house during the summer.

## Patios

It is the patio that is primarily designed as an extra outdoor living area. It may combine facilities for lounging, dining and cooking. Built-in barbecue systems complete with tiled food preparation areas, cupboards and chimneys, or the sophisticated bottled gas models with their spits and rotisseries, make some patios better equipped than many kitchens. The patio may even serve as 'bathroom' and health centre with an outdoor whirlpool spa or hot-tub — both of which take up very little room and, close to the house with suitable shelter and screening, can be enjoyed all year round.

Reflecting their major role as a living area, patios are frequently planned and decorated as carefully as any interior. Flooring may be concrete paving slabs, old stone (expensive unless broken pieces are used as 'crazy paving'), brick or ceramic tiles, or a mixture of several of these. All types are available in a huge variety of shapes and styles which can be mixed and matched to create patterns. Inexpensive pre-cast concrete slabs come in various shapes and shades that can be arranged to form designs such as the 'Dutch pattern', a concentric style using several sizes

that radiate out from a central square or rectangle. Some also imitate natural materials, and wet concrete can be dyed and stamped into a passable imitation of more expensive effects. Incorporating curves and circles into a patio paving design is a useful way to add interest and hide a limited or cramped area; so is mixing areas of different materials such as gravel with stone, wood chip with timber, or stone with brick. Equally popular and softer underfoot is timber decking, which may be constructed in soft- or hardwoods and stained to a natural timber glow or stylishly bleached grey or blue, Oriental red or soft olive green. Like bricks and tiles, lengths of timber can be arranged in smart herringbone and basketweave designs. Laid on the diagonal or in square sections at right angles to each other, they can also look very effective and may be used to play some interesting visual tricks. A great advantage of decking is its flexibility: it can be raised to any height and is easily constructed over large areas; and it can neatly incorporate handrails, matching planting beds, ornamental pools and hot-tubs.

Where a house opens directly on to a patio via French windows or other doors, the patio floor may be made to match that of the room inside, encouraging a feeling of space and continuity when the doors are open. Co-ordinating any accessories encourages the same effect, and so it makes sense to take your lead from the general style of your home when planning any area close to the house: if Oriental minimalism is your style, consider glazed Chinese ginger jars planted with bamboo and inset areas of raked sand or gravel; to complement a chintzy rustic interior, use a profusion of terracotta pots planted with herbs and cottage flowers.

*Left: Simple decking can make very effective bridges if the terrain is level.*

*Above: If unable to sink a pool, raise the level of the area around it.*

*Right: Large fountain fittings can also give a pond effect.*

*Far right: A domed recessed decorative fountain and pond at Hestercombe in Somerset.*

## Using water

A bold but stunning plan is to use water close to the house; a formal pool can be combined with decking or paving and creates pleasing reflections, especially if the property is of particular architectural merit and can be lit at night, spotlights positioned to throw into relief any particularly fine sills and mouldings. The pool can be butted up to the building or incorporated into a patio; a series of small pools on different levels adds interest and variety to any dull patio and can be linked with small waterfalls and weirs to provide the relaxing sound, as well as sight, of running water. Other moving water features make equally good patio companions: a free-standing fountain or wall-mounted waterspout, a watercourse dividing a large area into more intimate sections; or a formal raised pool, edged in brick, stone or timber to match the main patio construction. One interesting patio idea popular in Japan is to have a deep pool running directly under the house wall and into a room; this allows their lovely koi carp free access to warmer waters and produces a superb sense of continuity between house and garden.

*A patio garden screened off by clipped hedges at Hidcote Manor Gardens in Gloucestershire.*

## Screening and shelter

Patios need shelter and privacy, so screening is important: again this can be planned as decoratively as any wallcovering. Trellis, walling, fencing and screening can be plain and rustic or highly ornamental, and planted with a living curtain of foliage and flowers that will put on a changing display of shape and colour throughout the year. Some form of overhead shelter is useful on the patio, too, especially if it is used extensively as an outdoor dining area. It need only be partial to provide shade from hot sunshine or to filter light rain showers. A pergola structure is ideal and can be built from matching materials. It is usual to cover it with a suitable quick-growing vine or flowering climber, but it can be designed to incorporate light rattan or grass matting screens which can be pulled across the top when required. Alternatively, retractable awnings fixed to the house wall or giant umbrellas are equally flexible, and can be colour matched to container-grown blooms or outdoor furniture. Another idea is to stretch lengths of canvas over a simple wooden frame during summer.

*Top left: Stone walls and steps overgrown with moss and ivy to stunning effect.*

*Bottom left: Brick paving, steps and retaining wall blend together well in this small terrace garden.*

## Terraces

Where the paved area immediately by the house is raised and fairly long and narrow, it could be classed more as a terrace, particularly if formal in style with a predominance of paving and stone, Classical urns and statuary. A terrace tends to have a strong sense of symmetry, with shallow steps to centre or side leading down to the main garden from an elegant balustrade. Patios and terraces are most often sited at the rear of the house for privacy, and they form an introduction to the rest of the garden via a parapet, balustrade or low patio wall. However, they may be incorporated anywhere around the house that is practical for frequent and enjoyable use: at the front if space is restricted at the rear; or the side if this is the area that catches maximum sunshine. As a feature intended primarily for lounging and lingering, it makes sense to follow the sun rather than any rigid preconceptions as to where a patio ought to be. In villas and sometimes town houses, the patio is often incorporated on an upper level in order to enjoy a view as well as the usual benefits.

## Roof gardens

Many town- and city-dwellers without gardens use their roof as a space into which to expand their lifestyles. It has always been customary in densely populated centres like Katmandu, where no gardens exist, to plant roofs with flowers and even a lawn, and provide a place to hang out the washing, relax and chat to neighbours away from the noise and dust of the street sometimes several storeys below. Now the idea has spread to more sophisticated cities. If the building is strong enough to take the weight of heavy soil, plants and containers, then planting beds, lawns and even pools are possible. There are some elaborate high-rise roof gardens complete with trees, summer-houses, paths and pools, but these are very unusual. Shelter is essential as roofs tend to be extremely exposed, and light wooden screens and plastic netting specially designed for the purpose are available. For the same reason the hardiest plants should be selected, and everything must be well anchored. Screens and fences planted with tough climbers soon create a more amenable environment for people and other plants, and help counteract any feelings of vertigo. For practical reasons, the style of a roof garden should incorporate the lighter options used for patios:

timber decking which is easier to get up on a roof than heavy slabs; wooden or fibreglass containers; and the lightest folding garden furniture. Ease of access is also important for the regular use and maintenance of a roof garden.

*Top: A roof garden in which the chimney stack is celebrated.*

*Left: A gravel courtyard in Tring, Hertfordshire.*

*Above: Greenery cascading from a tiny roof garden on an English stone-and-hung-tile cottage.*

*Top left: Ancient courtyards in Rome.*

*Far left: A classic Caribbean courtyard in Havana, Cuba.*

*Near left: Even a modest, and none too sunny, courtyard can be given the grandeur of a formal garden by laying out a privet hedge parterre. Using containers allows for flexibility.*

## Backyards and courtyards

Other areas immediately round the house can pose practical problems. A tiny town backyard or court-yard is frequently gloomy and sunless, dominated by high walls, fencing and surrounding buildings. The cleverest owners turn it to advantage by creating a private, intimate area. Painting walls white helps bounce a lot more light into the area; much can also be done with mirrors and painted *trompe l'oeil* effects to create the impression of extra light and space. Paving or decking the complete area is another way to maximize space, with plants in raised beds or containers planned so as to maintain a good display all year. A great many evergreen species can be relied on in shadier conditions; adding highlights with a limited planting scheme of yellow, silver or white flowers and foliage lightens the effect. These are areas where vertical gardening comes into its own: climbers or pots pinned to trellis, hanging baskets, overhead wires and tall, free-standing supports all distract attention from the true size of the plot and create interest at every level.

Sometimes a yard can be claustrophobic but it often constitutes a sun-trap, especially in urban areas where surrounding buildings help raise the tempera-ture and cut out the cooling effect of winds. This can be turned to advantage with a collection of bright, sun-loving plants with a strong fragrance such as herbs and other Mediterranean species; or, in tem-perate climates, even offers the opportunity to grow a collection of outdoor exotics and tender subtropical plants.

## Front gardens

The area at the front of a building presents yet a different set of limitations and problems. Its role is primarily to show off the property to best advantage, providing visitors and the public with their first impression of the place. Thus it must be immaculately maintained at all times even though it has to cope with heavy traffic between the main gate or entrance and the front door, and often with pollution, vandalism and general wear and tear. Many schemes follow a symmetrical design, maintaining any architectural balance in the building: planting beds neatly arranged on either side of a path or steps – an obvious priority for providing clean, dry access to the front door; the plants themselves neatly matched in colour, height and type even in the informal cottage border. In towns, plants are often restricted to containers, making them easier to maintain and minimizing accidental damage from passers-by.

The front garden or yard often follows a traditional and familiar design such as neat suburban flower beds, echoing a Victorian mania for order and colour-co-ordinated bedding plants; or town pots and paving; or long herbaceous borders mixing ornamental flowers and vegetables like the monastery gardens of old. Gardens may be virtually identical along a street or around an estate following such preconditioned ideals. But occasionally the owners will be seized by a desire to express their individuality and will indulge in the unusual or outrageous: converting the whole area to a formal pool with access to the front door via a bridge, for example; adopting an off-beat theme such as ancient Egypt or, to the delight of local children, a collection of bright plastic gnomes. The area may even be played down to show off a particularly fine focal point such as a magnolia tree or a large piece of outdoor sculpture – a useful way to distract attention away from a less than lovely building.

*Opposite page: The quintessential English country cottage garden in Woodhouse, Leicestershire.*

*Left top: With just a little skill – and a great deal of patience – topiary can give the plainest exterior the look of an imposing manor house.*

*Left below: Topiary need not be ornate or elaborately sculptural to be effective.*

*Above: Profusion in a small front garden may be the only guarantee of privacy.*

# MARKING GROUND LINES

Front or rear, the paths that provide safe, dry access, and the fences, walls and screens that determine the extent and limits of its immediate grounds, add a great deal to the general style and atmosphere of a house. Priority then must be given to careful construction and strong, sensible materials, but this leaves plenty of scope for creativity and original design. Paths and passages need not lead directly to the door, but may follow a more circuitous route, taking in a few interesting features on the way. This is the principle adopted in the traditional Japanese tea garden, where a winding path of informal but deliberately spaced stepping stones encourages a leisurely pace and time for contemplation. Any paving materials can be used to create interesting path and stepping stone designs: sections of treated timber can be arranged in sophisticated decked walkways, or even raised to extend across planting beds and areas of water. Simple log slices may be used as stepping stones in a rustic setting. Bricks, paving slabs, flagstones and pre-cast concrete shapes offer even more decorative scope with so many shapes, colours and sizes to choose from, including interlocking designs, inserts and even cobbles and setts. Some turn-of-the-century town houses and villas traditionally have brightly coloured and bordered front paths created from ceramic tiles, as intricate and intriguing as an Oriental carpet. Other unusual treatments include mosaic patterns using coloured glass and even different-coloured pebbles arranged in geometric designs. For a more informal look, slabs or bricks can be laid straight on a level bed of sand and the gaps filled with soil and planted with mosses and hardy ground-cover plants. For a path leading to a cabin or into an informal part of a garden, bark chippings have a lovely woodland feel about them; stone chippings, gravel or pebbles are for smarter effects. Both need to be contained within the pathway with some kind of edging which might range from simple timber boards to old-fashioned moulded terracotta shapes or concrete lintels. Wire hoops and bent sticks are also useful for defining the edges of a path, and so is a low clipped hedge of evergreen box imitating the formal layout of medieval and monastery gardens.

Paths leading to the main door can be protected by taller hedging such as privet, box or some similar evergreen that can be neatly clipped so that it does not snag clothes; or shaded by a double row of pleached (interlaced) hornbeam or limes trained to form an arch; by fruit trees pruned and wired, espalier style, on either side; a pergola walkway or hooped metal framework covered in roses, wisteria, honeysuckle or other flowering climbers; or enclosed within a tunnel of ornamental stone, timber, brick or glass.

## Bridges, stepping stones and steps

Where stretches of water such as a pool or stream have to be negotiated, bridges and stepping stones can be organized with panache. Zigzagged sections of timber decking make a safe and stylish crossing, with rushes, reeds or other similar architectural water plants positioned as appropriate. A continuous length of decking makes an excellent low bridge that is

*Opposite page: Steps to a door in Great Brington, Northamptonshire.*

*Left (clockwise from top left):*

*Steps to a Californian house.*

*Elaborate external staircases to houses in the Old Quarter of Montreal in Canada's Quebec province.*

*A mosaic wall in Barcelona, Spain by Antonio Gaudí.*

*Wonderfully mysterious stone steps in a garden in Marske in the Yorkshire Dales.*

*A cast-iron staircase leading to the door of a house in Georgetown, Washington D.C.*

easily installed and allows the water to be viewed at close quarters; a more ornamental arched bridge is expensive but creates a grand focal point and a splendid approach to the banks beyond. These are generally constructed in timber or metal in Classical or Oriental styles to suit the garden, and can either be left natural to blend with their surroundings or painted a bright shade to stand out from them. Small informal streams can be treated far more modestly: a large slab of stone, an old tree trunk or a plank of timber, safely secured, makes an adequate and appropriate feature.

Changes of level mean that steps are often necessary, and when they lead up to a front door, patio or terrace they always seem to add a feeling of pomp and grandeur, however simple they are in style — from eighteenth-century stone and Victorian ceramic tiles, to the plain wooden steps up to a colonial residence. They may be smart and steep approaching a fine front door, flanked by ornamental wrought-iron railings or tubs of stately architectural green plants, old-fashioned iron boot scraper to the ready at the

*Above: Brick paving and steps leading to a house in Melbourne, Australia.*

*Near right: A decorative pebble-dash path leading to a house in Dublin, Eire.*

*Far right: A brick path edged with stone, leading to a 1920s 'Cape Dutch'-style house in North London's Bishop's Avenue.*

top of the flight. For all their stately elegance and imposing nature, they are fairly common in towns and cities. Traditionally a flight of stone steps leading up to the front door has been obligatory for town houses of any pretension since the late 1600s, even if the rise only merited two or three steps. By the nineteenth century, basement rooms and tall imposing residences meant a plethora of steep steps, often flanked by ornate iron railings and approached by a matching iron gate. Equally traditional are the wide,

be more informal: simply constructed in timber and climbing a bank or rise with bark chippings or gravel for treads; or retained by rustic log sections. A traditional feature of gardens in America, particularly the South, are curved grass steps like the ones to be seen at the Ladd House in New Hampshire. All steps are best provided with some form of handrail for safety, designed to suit the steps' own style and setting. Wrought iron, polished timber, pilastered stone, or concrete or timber uprights threaded with chains or sturdy ships' rope are all suitable.

## Driveways

As soon as a path is widened and strengthened to take vehicular traffic it becomes a driveway, which may lead directly to the front door, around to the rear or directly to the garage, depending on available space. Where the driveway is large and impressive, often with double access allowing cars to enter and exit, that expanse of gravel chippings, concrete or tarmac can look a little bleak, even when one of the more decorative coloured finishes is chosen. Clever planting around the perimeter can help to soften the effect and can also provide a good backdrop, screening off the road if hardy evergreen shrubs and trees are arranged according to breadth and height to create a dense landscaped effect. If space permits, a central feature makes a fine focal point and breaks up the area. A formal raised pool with fountain is traditional, but it might just as effectively be a handsome specimen tree (its roots protected within a small circular raised wall of brick or stone and planted with seasonal flowers or hardy ground-cover plants), a sundial, statue or sculpture.

*Above: A modern wooden extended canopy, making clever use of trellis supports.*

*Left (from top):*

*The entrance to a house in Melbourne, Australia.*

*A lattice canopy produces delightful light tracery beneath this Australian entranceway.*

*Classic herringbone brick paving.*

shallow steps that describe a graceful curve towards the stone-balconied entrance of a formal terrace or patio. Such features tend to be constructed in stone or concrete, softened by interesting sweeps, curves and decorative details or by the addition of plants. They became a favourite feature of eighteenth- and nineteenth-century landscape architects, and have remained popular for all sizes and styles of garden ever since.

Elsewhere in the grounds or garden, steps might

## Gates and garden doors

At the other end of the driveway, garden path or flight of steps is invariably a gate or garden door. Whether grand and electronically operated in wrought iron with great stone gateposts topped with an orb or eagle, or as simple as a wooden country wicket, and whether opening on to the road or street at the front, or fields at the back, its function is one of privacy and security and its general type and construction will reflect how far this is necessary. You may wish to bar prying eyes and unwelcome intruders, or simply keep livestock and stray animals out of the garden and pets and children inside for their own safety. In some areas, fully automatic, large metal gates completely screening the grounds and remotely operated may be a fact of life, whether out in the wilds or the centre of a city. Other areas can afford the luxury of more open-plan living, and ornamental gates in timber or wrought iron. There are also all kinds of ingenious devices offering the best of both worlds: a secure gate can still have ornamental peepholes or

trelliswork, glazed windows, metal grilles or fretwork effects through which to spy a fine view. A wrought-iron gate can be as simple as the front-garden gate to a suburban home with the occasional scroll and swirl detail, or as grand as the magnificent pairs of gates sometimes seen at the entrance to mansions, complete with family crest and other elaborate patterns worked into the design. Ironwork has been used for gates on grand estates and in towns and cities since the seventeenth century; by the eighteenth, even quite small houses would have plain cast-iron gates and railings. Timber gates tend to be more modest, although the art deco-style sunburst often seen on small wooden suburban gates in Britain has a certain charm. Generally, though, these gates are braced for strength in the manner of the traditional four- or five-barred field gate, simply having horizontal bars fastened to a 'z' frame. Variations include lightweight and attractive lapped panels, the familiar palings of the standard small garden gate, and close boarding for a heavier gate offering more privacy.

*Right: The Wachter Villa, near Antwerp in Belgium, by night.*

*Below (from left):*

*Ornamental detail on a gate to a liu yuan, or 'linger here', garden in China.*

*Nineteenth-century cast-iron railings and gate in Savannah, Georgia.*

## Boundaries: railings, fences, walls, screens and trellis

Security and privacy are again the incentive for erecting walls, fences and trellis around the limits of your land, but they can also be used to set off a building and give it a framework. To the detached house, standing alone, the boundary adds a comforting sense of order and security — without it a lone building on the edge of a shingle beach, for example, or in the middle of a prairie or wetlands, looks terribly exposed, even incongruous. For the terraced or semi-detached house, it is a way of establishing and defining territory, both visually and practically, and the level of privacy required will determine the choice and style of material. Those in country residences may even wish to adopt the eighteenth-century English invention, the ha-ha, which is an ingenious device whereby a fence set in a deep ditch kept animals out of the garden while allowing an uninterrupted view of the surrounding countryside.

Fencing and trellis are the quickest and easiest options and, in the plainest styles, can be the least expensive. Modern treatments mean that timbers last longer with minimum maintenance, and they can always be disguised with a quick-growing climber such as clematis, hops (*Humulus lupulus*) or Russian vine (*Polygonum baldschuanicum*). For those who prefer the strong architectural shape of a rigid structure to the rather shaggy, formless effect of covering foliage, there are more ornamental designs. Sturdy fencing is available in medieval and Victorian Gothic styles with turned posts, pinnacles and finials, trellis inserts and other decorative features. The Victorians and Edwardians, in particular, turned screening and fencing into a fine art, developing elaborate patterns and popularizing the rustic look.

Today, fencing comes in a wide range of standard types and designs, to be chosen according to need and location. Simple ranch-type post and rail fencing has an attractive open appearance and can be con-

structed using round rails or sawn boards, and yet it is very strong and – staggered in a zigzag arrangement or strengthened with mortice and tenon joints – can be used for stock maintenance. Equally strong but offering maximum privacy is the substantial close-boarded fence, which is also excellent as a low fence to protect plants as well as built high for good, permanent screening. It is particularly attractive in its feather-boarded form where tapered boards are neatly overlapped. Popular lapped panel fences (usually of larch) are also good for screening but they are not as strong as close-boarding. Their light weight makes them suited to roofs and balconies, but unless they are reinforced with slotted posts and concrete gravel boards, they are not strong enough to support climbing plants. Some panels are not overlapped but interwoven, creating an attractive design and texture.

Panels and close-boarding create shade; but more open post and rail fencing will not keep out small animals. If you need to incorporate both facilities, the solution is chestnut paling, which is modest but attractive with pointed, rounded or feather-edge-topped palings. Also popular is 'hit-and-miss' style post and board fencing where the boards are nailed on alternate sides of the post, leaving a gap between them of around 15cm/6in. This offers privacy and support for climbing plants, while allowing light through to adjacent low-growing plants. From these standard types, more decorative ideas are easily explored and can be frequently seen around more imaginative exteriors: timber stained or painted to match the colour of door and window frames, or incorporating cut-outs and 'windows'; or the top sculptured into a curved rather than a straight profile, producing a continuous scalloped effect. The posts themselves can also be decorated, topped with balls, finials or flat caps.

Wire and netting also come in a wide range of styles for security, partial screening and plant support. PVC-coated chain link is particularly strong and

*Top left: A wooden fence in Guilford, Connecticut, painted iron-red to match the brick and woodwork of the house.*

*Bottom left: Elegantly undulating white-painted wooden picket fence and ornamental gatepost in Essex, Connecticut.*

*Above: Classically simple white-painted picket fence and gate to a late-eighteenth-century weatherboard house in Essex, Connecticut.*

*The gates to the garden of a gabled Victorian Hampshire manor house have been slightly curved to frame one of the best views of the building.*

impenetrable and is available in a wide selection of heights and a choice of colours. Merely to keep out road traffic or delineate a boundary, a simple wooden post and chain fence is often enough in an urban setting. Railings serve a similar purpose: they are strong and secure yet allow free vision, and they can also be extremely decorative. Never seeming to lose favour with either grand or small town houses, they have remained popular for almost three hundred years. Quite plainly constructed outside the smallest terrace house, they might have the addition of matching iron balustrades, spear tops, spikes and pine-cone decorations outside larger, grander houses. Early ironwork might be beautifully wrought; later examples dating from the eighteenth century onwards could equally well be hammered or cast, a cheaper option popular for more modest homes.

For privacy without maximum security, lightweight screens are an excellent way to keep out cold winds and prying eyes, particularly around a patio, front garden or roof garden. They might be made of bamboo for an Oriental look, or of timber, or rush, reed, or willow hurdles; brushwood bound together with wire is another rustic option. All are useful for adding new colours and textures to a garden or patio scheme and are quickly and easily erected. Surprisingly perhaps, an equal range of effects is possible using walling, a far more permanent and secure form of screening offering both excellent privacy and a deterrent to burglars, depending on how substantial and high it is.

Walls can be matched to the main fabric of the building to encourage a sense of co-ordination and continuity, using second-hand materials if necessary. Bricks come in many shades from the russets through to almost black; there are also decorative concrete patio blocks and imitations of natural stone for a similar choice of decorative designs around a modern dwelling. Any of these can be built into pillars and columns, incorporate peep-holes, stone or wooden cartwheels, shells and stones, a mosaic of coloured

tiles, castellated tops, chains, rails and grilles for variety and mixed effects. Other features can be built in: alcoves and arches, seating bays, raised beds, shelves for plant pots and seats themselves. Leaving occasional spaces and filling with compost creates plant pockets for dry-loving rock plants such as stonecrop (*Sedum acre*) and houseleeks (*Sempervivum*). Bricks offer a choice of bonded designs, depending on whether the course is laid end-on or lengthways. To add brightness to a dull backyard, bland concrete or brick walls can be painted with *trompe l'oeil* designs or light-coloured paint. For more of a rustic look, old stone makes a marvellous rough-textured wall, either cemented or using the dry-stone walling technique: a skilled dry-stone waller can incorporate herringbone patterns and other interesting details. It helps to use local stone wherever possible in the garden to encourage a natural look: in areas where flints occur, for example, a wall might be faced with them in decorative rows.

For those with time and patience, hedging is one of the best screening materials. When it has thickened up, a hedge offers good security, too, especially a prickly variety like holly or thorn. An eighteenth-century idea was to combine walls with hedges, maybe planting a hedge on top of an earth wall, reinforced with stonework; or building up a mound of soil for the hedge behind an existing wall to produce a similar effect. Copper beech is outstanding for its stunning copper-red foliage, and equally impressive is the dark green formality of one of the small-leaved evergreens such as privet, box and yew which can be clipped into smart shapes and archways. Box and yew are very slow growers, and box is most often used as low hedging between flower beds, although its dense habit also makes it suitable for mazes. For a much quicker effect, the evergreen *Thuja* makes a dense screen within a couple of years; and thorn, field maple, holly and gorse can all be used to grow a country-style, more rustic hedge.

*Above (clockwise from left):*

*Polesden Lacey in Surrey.*

*Gate to a walled garden, Market Overton, Wiltshire.*

*A garden wall in Burnham Market, Norfolk.*

*A brick wall with ornamental iron panels.*

*An old wooden gate in Rutland, Leicestershire.*

*A dry stone wall in Devon.*

*Topiary at a gate in Horringer, Suffolk.*

are not available, or in areas of the garden where a self-supporting feature is required.

Pergolas are an excellent decorative device for adding height to a scheme or providing overhead shade for a patio or similar paved area. They can also be used to create covered walkways, a series of arches or special plant supports for displaying roses, clematis or wisteria. They are frequently designed to be supported on one side by the house wall, and if further privacy or shelter is required — say for a hot-tub or an eating area — the other sides can be screened using bamboo, louvres or lattice fencing. The supports can be constructed from stone, concrete or brick pillars, rustic larch or chestnut, sawn timber or metal poles; and topped with a horizontal arrangement of cross pieces. The most attractive arrangement cantilevers the crosspieces out over the side of the structure, providing extra shade and a wider support for plants.

A similar arrangement can be constructed from

*Left: An arched hedge set off by a low white-painted picket fence in East Hampton, Long Island, New York.*

*Above: A wooden gate with canopy in Essex, Connecticut.*

*Right: Metal arches can be used to train plants over the entranceway.*

## Pergolas, arches and other plant supports

All these screening effects are useful, not just as a means of marking out and protecting boundaries, but also within a garden scheme to divide it into special areas or new sections, to add a sense of mystery, hide an eyesore or make a small garden seem larger than it really is. They not only work as garden dividers, but also add interesting height and bulk to the final effect. Staggered breaks of hedging or trellis can add a sense of width to a long, narrow garden, for example. Other kinds of 'hard landscaping' in timber or metal may also be useful for contributing more body and height to a garden and linking a building to the landscape. These structures can be free-standing or attached to the house, and provide a firm vertical support for climbing and trailing plants where fence and trellis

trellis, rustic timber, wire or metal hoops, usually designed to support climbing roses but equally useful for any kind of attractive climber. This may be plainly constructed or highly ornate, depending on how much of it will be left exposed, and can be used to create a single arch or a tunnel effect, or even a lean-to arrangement along a side passage or attached to a building. An archway always makes a fine feature, whether as an entrance to a new part of the garden, a central focal point or as part of a wall or fence and incorporating a timber or wrought-iron gate. A stone or brick arch always looks particularly handsome, especially when well weathered or coloured with mosses and lichens. Old archways sometimes include pithy inscriptions or wall-mounted sundials, helping to attract attention to this fine architectural feature.

## EXTERIOR ACCESSORIES

Like the best interior schemes, a successful and good-looking exterior relies on a careful and inspired choice of accessories and finishing touches. These can set a style or reinforce it, capturing exactly the right period detail or creating a style all of their own. It is worth taking the time and trouble to assemble such details carefully, to give thought not just to their design and the material of which they are made, but also to how and where they might be positioned. This is especially true of the immediate area around the house and on paved features such as a patio or terrace, where plants and ornaments are essential for adding character and softening the hard architectural lines of surrounding surfaces.

### Tricks of the eye

First, it may be necessary to organize a few visual tricks to set the scene and perhaps make a few visual alterations to a less than perfect canvas. The shape and style of patio areas and the organization of major hard landscaping elements, such as walls, fences, pergolas and screens, may have already gone some way towards making the area look wider, longer or more interesting than it seemed at first. But there are other tricks you can borrow from the interior decorator and professional landscape designer. For example, mirrors can be used outdoors to great effect, especially in small enclosed areas. A couple of strategically placed mirrors reflecting to infinity a medley of foliage, flowers and entrances will create the impression that the garden goes on for ever. Mirrors can be used with equal success set into an archway, entrance, or behind trellis; or where they can reflect a path or doorway, perhaps framed and disguised by a surrounding curtain of ivy or similar evergreen creeping or trailing plant. Water can be cleverly used in the garden to similar effect. Its naturally reflective nature makes spaces seem larger by reproducing light and sunshine from above, as well as duplicating reflections of surrounding trees and plants. Timber decking just above the ground and overhanging a shallow stretch of water will make the water appear to extend much further and be deeper than it is. For even more impact, mirrored glass set behind the arch of a fake bridge will give the strong impression that the water does indeed flow under it and out at the other side.

It is not always necessary to use mirrors or water to play visual games: a false door or archway set into a wall or at the end of a path within a small garden scheme will suggest something interesting beyond it; as will the total illusion presented by an outdoor *trompe l'oeil* painting. In a gloomy basement backyard a simple trick is to paint walls white or pale yellow to help generate an impression of light and sunshine, but in a dull or difficult location it can be worth being a little more adventurous and indulging in an ambitiously artistic effort: perhaps realistically suggesting a view beyond a blank door; a clump of perennially flowering blooms up a dull wall; a painted cat and milk bottles waiting patiently by the back door; or the hens you always wanted painted in full colour on the backyard fence.

## Lighting

Outdoor lighting can also be relied upon to perform a little optical wizardry, but as already discussed in the previous chapter, it can be important from a practical and safety angle too. Good lighting along paths and driveways and illuminating front and back doors is essential after dark, to provide safe and easy access. This can be done by means of overhead spotlights, floodlights or ornamental spiked lights and lanterns at intervals along verges and flower beds. The building itself may be floodlit to display its best architectural features; or, more traditionally, be fitted with antique or good reproduction Victorian or Edwardian lanterns – an old iron street lamp is a popular choice for the gardens of houses of all periods. For convenience, lights could be operated on a time switch or by remote control from house or car. Lighting up the immediate area around the house at night will also deter burglars, and heat-sensitive lights are available which switch on should anyone approach.

Equally important for safety is the need to light any bridges or stepping stones if the garden is to be used after dark. Lights can be clipped unobtrusively along the underside of low timber bridges, or lanterns strung overhead to illuminate more elaborate arched styles. A fairly sophisticated scheme should be planned for patio areas too, so that full use can be made of their facilities. Soft lights hidden overhead in pergola foliage can create a suitably moody atmosphere for seating and dining areas, with some form of spotlight provid-

*Top: Working gas lights outside a nineteenth-century house in Georgetown, Washington D.C.*

*Above: Porch lights on a late-nineteenth-century house in San Antonio, Texas.*

*Right: An extravagantly romantic Victorian conservatory gas lamp fitting.*

ing safe, practical illumination of any barbecues, hot-tubs or pools. Lighting can also be used purely for effect, making a spectacle of the house or subtly lighting up the garden in order to create a wonderful night-time panorama best viewed from the patio, terrace or rooms inside. Strongly architectural plants and trees look good with their shapes highlighted from below, as do statues, fountains and other ornamental features. Lighting can be purely temporary, too, and a party is a good excuse for experimenting with ornamental candles: adopting the Victorian idea of stringing them in the trees in coloured glass lanterns looks very pretty. For soft, low-level lighting, Oriental bamboo flares (with refillable oil reservoirs) stuck into flower beds look very effective.

## Containers and ornamental plant forms

Plants are often grown in containers or raised beds close by a building, where the area is frequently hard-surfaced and they need some protection from people passing by on a regular basis. Choice of plants is naturally important, and careful consideration must be given to their height, shape and colour, but the tubs and containers are equally so, and should be matched, for style and material, both to the building and to their immediate environment. This is not difficult, given the vast range to choose from, so that terracotta, old wooden tubs or barrels and real or imitation stone may be chosen for rustic-style patios, and reproduction stone and lead urns for a formal terrace. Panelled Versailles tubs are always a smart match for a grand scheme, either in a natural timber finish or painted sparkling white, while baskets and Chinese glazed jars are perfect for an Oriental atmosphere. For a modern scheme, concrete planters come in a wide choice of heights and sizes for easy container landscaping; use lightweight fibreglass for roof gardens

and balconies. Happy traditionalists have their pick of real and good reproduction container designs, from terracotta styles – little changed since the Romans – to seventeenth-century wooden metal-hooped tubs, as well as the elaborate patterns and designs in metal and earthenware developed by the Victorians and still with us today.

As a rule, it is not a good idea to mix styles and materials too much, since this can make a scheme look muddled. Container plants look best in closely assembled groups of varying heights and sizes, but employing some common theme such as timber, terracotta or colour. Pots matched in size and type look good placed on either side of the front door, at the top of a flight of steps or an entrance to a terrace or patio. With steps and wider porch areas, a collection of similar or matching plants can make a fine display. Where space is limited, forget all about symmetry and position plants on one side of the door or steps only, to prevent them being a nuisance, getting damaged or blocking access.

*Left: The classic front-door treatment of twin box trees in matching containers.*

*Above: Front-door containers need not simply contain green shrubs or trees. Seasonal planting, using flowering shrubs for height, can be splendidly effective.*

*Above: An ornamental horse trough in the Ladew Topiary Garden near Baltimore, Maryland.*

*Near right: An ornamental urn used as a centrepiece.*

*Middle right: The shape of the greenery echoes the curve of the wings of an eagle on a raised plinth.*

*Far right: A statue of a reclining mother with child brings great peace to this small garden.*

## Statuary, sculpture and ornaments

Finishing off an outdoor scheme with a few well-placed ornaments, or using a large sculpture or statue as a focal point, can lift the whole area out of the ordinary or add the crowning touch to a carefully thought-out design. Classical statuary can be original or copies, in marble, stone or lead, depicting Greek and Roman deities, cavorting nymphs, cherubs and all manner of figures, cornucopia and decorative urns, as found in the grand gardens of the early eighteenth century with their balustrades, niches and pedestals. Modern statuary and sculpture range from the whimsical (life-size stone piglets to root around the corners of the patio; or a bronze girl designed to dip her toe in the shallows of a pool) to many more

traditional figures or abstract designs and surreal giant fruits. This type of feature needs the right background to set it off to best advantage: either a central position where it can attract attention as a focal point, or placed against a suitably neutral backdrop such as a curtain of evergreen foliage, a mellow wall or screened corner.

Ornaments are most likely to be positioned on parapets and in niches, or at ground level among containers, on steps, beside pools and decorating doors and entrances. They might comprise terracotta baskets and bronze animals, small urns and giant amphora for a Mediterranean feel; or where a Japanese-style theme is being encouraged, ornaments with an Oriental touch such as stone buddhas, lanterns, bowls and anything made of bamboo.

Some ornamental items are also of a practical nature. The Victorian cast-iron boot scraper serves its purpose by the front door, and a sundial or birdbath makes an excellent and attractive central feature in a formal scheme. Sundials can be wall-mounted too, adding interest to a wall or dull façade. Other items that may also be fastened to the wall of a building include carved stone or terracotta heads, sometimes spouting water into a small pool, gargoyles, lions' heads, plaques and carvings. A 'found' object can make an excellent ornament: for example, an ancient wooden wheelbarrow or kitchen range planted with flowers, an old fashioned birdcage, or simply a collection of large, sea-washed pebbles.

Some plants can be classed almost as ornaments: certainly miniature topiary forms can be treated and positioned in this way. Small-leaved pot-based evergreens, usually box, may be clipped into formal shapes such as animals or, more likely on this scale, geometric forms such as orbs and cubes, cones, pyramids and spirals can look especially impressive in matched pairs, in rows along a path or up a flight of steps. Other ornamental plant forms that can be used in a similar creative way include vigorous climbers like one of the ornamental ivies; or a sweet-scented evergreen honeysuckle, trained up a container-mounted support to produce a leafy, hooped, shaped or even orbed effect.

*Left and above (clockwise from top left):*

*Tiny stone-shaped carved sheep dotted round a tree.*

*An elegant Classical urn garlanded with wisteria.*

*An urn raised on a plinth to give a focal point.*

*Neptune emerging from a water garden.*

*Giant carved acorns or pineapples are favourite devices for garden ornament.*

*Sculpted figures and detailing are all the more effective when barely emerging from the undergrowth.*

## GARDEN SHELTERS

Some kind of ornamental garden shelter, often in the form of a timber frame covered with climbing plants, has always been a popular way of taking refuge from the rain and hot sunshine without having to go indoors. By the sixteenth century these arbours or bowers had become large and elaborate, extended into long tunnel-like affairs, and they remained popular until the eighteenth century when landscape architects abandoned them for grander devices and designs. They were really the forerunners of today's pergolas and summerhouses, although they were revived by the Victorians who liked to grow dense evergreens over an ornate metal framework. Some old timber-framed arches with bench seats inside are still to be found in gardens around America, very close in design to the original medieval types. Sometimes a natural feature would be converted into an arbour: there are several existing examples in the UK of ancient clipped yews complete with seats inside their huge, hollow bulk – at Powys Castle, for instance.

*Top: The gazebo atop the steps at the end of the Long Walk in Hidcote Manor Gardens, Gloucestershire.*

*Left: The trompe l'oeil painted interior of the summerhouse in the grounds of King Henry's Hunting Lodge in Hampshire, which was the home of the internationally celebrated interior designer John Fowler.*

## Arbours and gazebos

Arbours are now enjoying another revival, especially in small gardens. They are usually made from sections of ornamental trellis constructed to create an enclosure, rather like a high-backed garden seat with an arched roof. They are tall but narrow, and one or even two can be fitted snugly against a boundary wall or fence on the smallest site. The beauty of this arrangement is that it can be designed to suit any type of patio or garden scheme, depending on the style of trellis used, and can be left plain and varnished or stained a subtle blue, grey or russet according to personal taste.

The gazebo is a similar structure which has long been a part of the Classical or formal garden: it usually comprises an ornate, free-standing but open structure in wood or metal, usually circular or square in shape with a pretty pointed roof. It is designed to be almost completely smothered in flowering climbers to provide a pleasant place to sit and enjoy the sun, or views of the rest of the garden. It is frequently positioned on a formal lawn as a decorative feature, and its natural attractiveness makes it a good focal point and an ideal feature for the small garden where any major structures have to remain on show. A similar but more enclosed effect can be created using a small free-standing circular or hexagonal conservatory, a useful solution where lack of space prohibits installing a larger one, either adjoining the house or elsewhere in the garden.

*Top right: A delightful little cottage built by John Nash around 1811 in Blaise Hamlet, near Bristol, Avon. It is almost dwarfed by its dovecot and ornamental chimneys and has a tiny built-in niche for a garden shelter just big enough for a bench.*

*Right: Even utilitarian objects like the wood-shed can make decorative features.*

*An orangery in Westbury on Severn, Gloucestershire.*

## Chalets, summerhouses and pavilions

Where space is limited, a larger garden building can work hard for its keep by being good looking enough to keep on show, while fulfilling several functions. A summerhouse can be used for storing tools, furniture, toys and other garden paraphernalia as well as providing a pleasant place to sit or shelter. Summerhouses should be positioned where they will face the best of the sun: some can be revolved to face it at all times, while others incorporate a verandah and patio area to make the most of finer weather. Styles and sizes vary enormously and, if money is no object, virtually anything can be designed to fit in with a particular garden look or to match the style of the main house. Popular options are comfortable, rustic-looking cabins and chalets which can look quite attractive tucked away at the end or in the corner of even a small garden. Other ready-made designs include pavilion-style buildings with folding doors and integral verandahs. For more central sites, since chalets and pavilions are often designed to stand in a corner or to the rear of a garden, there are also many styles of octagonal and hexagonal building, glazed to create a greenhouse-summerhouse hybrid ideally suited to small gardens that would not normally have room for both functions.

For something a little more stylish, a summerhouse made to the owner's own requirements can be a perfect excuse to indulge a fantasy. It may be a miniature pagoda reached via a Chinese-style bridge in a small town garden; a rustic log cabin studded with giant fir cones on a country estate; or a tiny black and white cottage complete with thatched roof. The excuse for these may be that they are to amuse the children, but these sophisticated forms of playhouse delight adults too, and few are reluctant to use them as shelter, tea-house or retreat.

Alternatively, when looking for an unusual style and a touch of elegance, you could take your lead from the well-sculpted landscapes of the eighteenth

*Top left: The 'Orangerie' in the grounds of Bradley Hall, Staffordshire.*

*Far left: A tiny thatched summerhouse, built in the 1950s, by the pond in the Hermitage Gardens, Warwickshire.*

*Near left: The 'figure of charity' shrine adorning the blind end of a cottage in Sir Clough Williams-Ellis's Portmeirion village in Gwynedd.*

century, when designers favoured a mock Greek temple some distance from the main house and fully furnished with table and chairs (and often a painted mural on the wall featuring a suitably idyllic scene) for stylish summer dinner parties. If there is room, it is an idea that could be copied quite easily using today's fake stone and marble architectural effects. Or perhaps you would like to follow the Victorians, who favoured the folly, an idiosyncratic building in the grounds of a house, usually maintained as a kind of 'den' or retreat for the owner. Elaborately constructed with eccentric towers and turrets, these often had two storeys with an outside staircase, and imitated whatever architectural style the owner most favoured.

Whatever the size, style and grandeur of a garden shelter, it is a good idea to provide some form of dry access – usually a path or stepping stones – between it and the main building. This is particularly important where, with garden space often at a premium, even the smartest summerhouses have taken on a new dual role. Suitably positioned, they can sometimes double as changing rooms for a nearby swimming pool or, with a mobile phone and electricity point, make an ideal away-from-it-all study or office for days worked at home.

Sometimes a property includes existing outbuildings that, if solidly built from traditional materials, can often be attractively and usefully converted to a new purpose, despite considerable neglect and decay. These usually adjoin, or are close to, the main building, which makes them ideal home extensions, pool houses, exercise rooms or storage areas to relieve the burden on home and garden. Whether they were originally barns, stabling, *pigeonnier* or stall boxes, it helps to retain as much of their original character as possible.

Paved areas, paths and plants can be arranged so that these buildings blend successfully into the garden scheme as well as with the house itself.

# EXTERIOR TREATMENTS

*Paint magic at work on an exterior:*
*the walls have been dragged in two shades of greeney-blue,*
*the door columns marbled and the*
*main window surround has stencilled decoration.*

Paint as an external finish for buildings has a history reaching far back into antiquity, though tantalizingly little has survived the centuries of exposure to show us what type of paints and pigments were used, and how they were applied.

Clues suggests that the ancient world admired strong, vivid colours, boldly combined; these seem to have been customary on important buildings, temples, palaces and the villas of the rich. Paint was a means of display rather than the surface protection we primarily think of it as today. It was used over materials we would leave unadorned, like stone and marble; classical Greek temples are thought to have been as brightly coloured as the statues they housed. The first sizeable remains of exterior treatments were excavated at Pompeii, the Roman town engulfed by lava just before the Christian era; enough exterior colour remains to suggest that paints, or coloured renders, were by then within reach of ordinary citizens.

Coloured renders would have evolved naturally from primitive daub or adobe finishes, using coloured clays found locally. By Roman times, with their technological prowess, these had developed in the direction of the refined stucco which has been the pride of Italian craftsmen ever since. Adding pigments to the final rendered surface of a building gives a more durable exterior colour than a superficial layer of paint; paint, on the other hand, went on quickly, cost much less, and allowed more freedom with colour. Often the two were combined, bands of coloured paint round windows and doors, enlivening the muted earthy shades of various types of render. Fashions change slowly in exterior treatment and direct descendants of

antique prototypes can still be found in many parts of the world today.

After a century of experimenting with a wide variety of 'modern' external paints and finishes – from pebble-dash to wood stains – the signs are that the wheel is turning full circle and that the advantages of traditional – often ancient – types of paint are being rediscovered, and appreciated, in the light of current 'green' or conservationist thinking.

*A house in the Greek island of Santorini.*

## LIMEWASH

Anyone who has stayed on one of the Greek islands will have been struck by the dazzling white of their painted buildings, stunningly clear against the blues of sea and sky, adorned with purple bougainvillaea and shutters painted blue and green.

This pristine white is developed by repeated – often yearly – applications of limewash, one of the most ancient paints, made basically from slaked lime and water. Lime is obtained by calcining limestone, to create a brittle white solid called quicklime, which is then slaked with water in lime pits to drive

off the caustic element. This creates hydrated lime, the main constituent of the sparkling white traditional 'whitewash' used for centuries by cottage dwellers in regions as far apart as Mexico, Greece and Ireland. It is usually made from locally available lime and is a cheap way of 'doing the place over' each spring.

The main disadvantage, in a modern context, of this simple treatment is that it is most effective as the final layer of a lime-based building system, ie over bricks or stones held together with lime mortar, and finished, perhaps with a lime-based render. These are all excellent traditional building materials popular with conservationists today because they allow buildings to settle without cracking, give a softer organic texture, and let masonry 'breathe'. A limewash finish actually strengthens the lime in underlying mortar and render. It is only under these traditionally occurring conditions that the final limewash arrives at its utmost brilliance of colour. However, it can be used over modern paints provided these are first sized to seal them, but there is a loss of brilliance.

Limewash tinted with lime-proof pigments, mostly earth colours, gives exterior finishes of exceptionally radiant colouring – visibly pure, with a lively translucency of tone quite different from opaque colours. Coloured limewash becomes richer with each successive coat, and has the additional charm of mellowing with age and weathering well. Coloured limewash is normally applied over a lime render, the whiteness of which adds to the glow of the final result.

In the bucket, limewash is a thin fluid and needs frequent stirring in use. It is usually applied with a large coarse-bristled or

*A range of traditional limewash colours.*

## STUCCO

Stucco as we know it today, smoothly coating Regency terraces or Italianate nineteenth-century villas, is chiefly the legacy of John Nash, the architect and speculative builder, who made stucco rendering fashionable and desirable in the early 1800s.

Stucco was versatile; it could be lined out to imitate ashlar joints in stone, and frescoed in grey-tawny shades resembling fashionable Bath stone; it could be rusticated below a string course; or it could be smoothly finished and painted. Its popularity was, in part, a reaction against the uniformity of stock bricks used for most terrace housing through the eighteenth century; it also served as a useful disguise for inferior materials and workmanship.

Stucco is an Italian word, meaning plaster or render, and Italian builders have led the world in the use of this versatile substance — essentially a refined render, using lime mortar and washed sand — since Roman times. They developed an astonishing variety of finishes and techniques, often with regional variations.

To make stucco 'alla veneziana' for instance, surfaces are first coated with a 'sottofondo' of lime and sand, or 'calce', and then finished with one or more layers of a finer grade of 'calce' made with finer sand. These layers are applied and worked over with steel tools resembling paint scrapers to give an exceptionally hard integrated, smooth finish. The finest stucco of all, 'marmorino', uses marble dust mixed with the finishing layer of 'calce'

fibre brush, slapped on with broad loose strokes.

White limewash looks water-clear on application, becoming white as it dries; while a peculiarity of some tinted washes is that they 'go on' quite a different shade from the final result when dry. 'Copperas', for instance, is a thin pond-green shade on first application, drying to a soft glowing tawny orange. Limewash colours have a special appropriateness on many old buildings, and, if the use of limewash is impracticable, it is worth studying the colours illustrated here to match them as nearly as possible when using a modern exterior paint.

## DISTEMPER

One of the simplest and most ancient of paints, distemper is made by binding powdered chalk, of varying degrees of fineness, with organic animal glue thinned with water. Untinted, its natural colour is a creamy white; tinted, it gives matt, powdery, highly saturated colour, which can be pastel, bright, or deep toned according to the pigment chosen, and the amount added.

Distemper dries with an almost velvety texture which is visually highly appealing. However, it does have a tendency to rub off, which makes it a better choice for bedrooms than much frequented hallways or kitchens. Its main use has been as an inexpensive and easily applied interior paint, but by adding enough oil, or other constituents, to make an emulsion, distempers can be made reasonably weather-proof.

The Falun red used on so many wooden buildings throughout Scandinavia is a version of distemper — or was in its traditional form — often using rye-flour paste as well as a host of different 'secret' ingredients which varied from one person — or place — to another. The old Falun red, tinted with red oxide from the Scandinavian copper mines, was a preservative for wooden structures as well as a decorative finish — one coat is said to have lasted ten years! The soft brown red colour is a remarkably sympathetic ingredient in the somewhat monotonous green of the Scandinavian countryside, especially when detailed in white for windows and cornices.

*Houses in Bath, Avon dating from 1805.*

over a 'sottofondo' made from crushed bricks and tiles, called 'cotto'. The surface is then finished with a hot iron to bring out a shine. Marmorino is exceptionally water-resistant, a great advantage in Venetian buildings facing on to canals.

These stucco finishes were used both inside and out, often coloured with pigments added to the final layer of 'calce'. In common with other lime-based finishes, these stucco surfaces age gracefully, picking up 'a crystal-line brightness' in the words of one Italian writer, or oxidizing 'to a colour of sea shells found on the shore. These are . . . characteristics of the material that cannot be created in any other way.'

It would be superfluous to paint stucco of such quality, but the coarser types more commonly found outside Italy are an ideal surface for paint, whether traditional lime-wash or modern exterior grade paints. Over a lime-based stucco it is common sense to use a limewash where possible, because it will 'feed' and strengthen the stucco, as well as give exceptionally distinguished colours.

The mysterious material, Coade Stone, an artificial stone which became immensely fashionable in the late eighteenth century and was popularized by the Adam brothers, seems to have been a development of stucco. Another variant, incorporating marble chips – and highly polished – gives the artificial marble known as 'scagliola'. Despite their labour-intensiveness, and initial cost, many of these stucco derivatives are currently being revived – as much for their intrinsic quality as their exceptional life span.

## COB WALLS

Cob, daub and adobe are all variants of the most primitive exterior coating material of all – local clay mud, sometimes with a little straw, animal hair or other fibre added to help bind it. This was then plastered over a frame of timber and woven bark, or wattles, to make a solid bulk, often a foot or more thick. With these 'found' materials, a crude – but wind- and weather-proof – dwelling could be constructed quite rapidly for next to no cost. A thatched roof, projecting out over the cob walls, would help keep off the worst of the rain. In other parts of the world, turf roofs, complete with spring wild flowers, might be used instead. Cob has a rounded tea-cosy look, as much part of its rural setting as a plump boletus.

Despite cob's seeming vulnerability to wet climates, cob cottages – it always remained a humble vernacular material – have frequently lasted in surprisingly good repair, for centuries. This is one reason why today's new breed of cottage dwellers are increasingly interested in repairing or restoring their charming rustic homes in the same materials.

*A door in Mauritania.*

Clay, as potters and pond makers know by experience, is surprisingly waterproof. A bed of puddled clay was often used to create a garden pond or farmyard water-hole for livestock.

Patching and repairing cob walls with modern concrete is not only aesthetically unfortunate, since it introduces an alien hardness and rigidity, but can also set up unexpected structural chain reactions, with the grafted-on substance conflicting – like an organ transplant – with the original structure and system. Today's open-minded approach to traditional materials and building techniques is encouraging people everywhere to reappraise even the simplest of vernacular traditions. This from a latter-day standpoint usually confirms that ancient practice was wiser than even its proponents realized.

*Decorated mud walls in Ghana.*

*Houses in Appledore, Devon.*

*One of the 'painted ladies' of Old San Francisco.*

*An unusual treatment of exposed timber frame in Germany.*

## EXTERIOR ACCENT COLOURS

The quickest way to smarten up the appearance of a building is to re-paint the exterior detailing, window frames, front door, porch, barge-boards, railings and so forth. Home owners have tended to see this necessary maintenance as an opportunity to stamp their own taste and personality on a house which may otherwise be indistinguishable from its neighbours.

The practice of picking out exterior detail in contrasting paint colours seems to have followed the general introduction of softwood joinery around the late seventeenth century. Soft wood, like pine and deal, needs to be protected against damp and frost otherwise, it soon cracks and rots. Lead paints,

which virtually cover surfaces with a metal skin, were the standard choice for protecting exposed softwood detail for many centuries, until their use was banned for health reasons. Until zinc white was introduced in the early nineteenth century, white lead was the best white pigment available, and it formed the base – mixed with other colours, or on its own – for most exterior paint. It is exceptionally long lasting, with a lifespan of decades rather than years. Indeed there are examples of lead-painted garden pavilions well over a hundred years old. It was also, like most traditional paints, aesthetically pleasing. It developed a soft patina with time and wore away subtly by surface erosion, instead of cracking and flaking off like more recent exterior paints. The ridgy texture of lead paint, when applied with a coarse bristled brush, is thought to have been the inspiration for the decorative paint finish called 'dragging'.

Today, with the banning of lead paint for all but historic buildings, the most durable and satisfactory exterior paint is a gloss paint with a high linseed oil content, applied over a basic system consisting of wood primer, undercoat, and 'split' coat – ie an intermediate coat made up of half undercoat and half gloss. The laboriousness of applying this sort of paint finish has led to increased use of lower maintenance alternatives, notably the hardwood joinery finished with protective stains, which are becoming standard in recent housing. Good protective wood stains have been developed in Scandinavia, where softwood is the prime building material and protecting it against punishing winters has always been a central preoccupation.

## PAINTING WINDOWS

The earliest types of windows, usually of a lead lattice filled with tiny glass panes and set in a rigid stone or timber framework, did not require paint to protect them. It was not until softwood sashes became standard throughout the better class of housing, during the seventeenth century, that paint was commonly used on windows.

White paint – but the softer greyish white of white lead – was the most popular colour

*An unusual primary colour treatment on the detailing on houses in Montreal, Canada.*

right up to the end of the Palladian era, contrasting 'fairly and cleanly' with the rosy brick of the seventeenth century as well as the greyish yellow of eighteenth-century London stocks. Other colours were used too: darker browns and russets, on less prosperous house fronts (because these colours were both cheaper and longer-lasting); stone colour; lead colour (lead white with a little indigo) on grander façades; gold leaf on the grandest and showiest of all (like Chatsworth, seat of the Dukes of Devonshire). However, white or pale colours predominated, liked for their sparkle and the way they brought out the subtle rhythm of fenestration.

The neo-Classical movement, around the end of the eighteenth century, dreamed of

*A selection of the colours traditional to lead paints.*

## PAINTING METALWORK

Of the various sorts of metalwork which might have been used on exteriors from the seventeenth century (lead for pipes and gutters, copper for decorative roofing), wrought-iron, and later cast-iron, were the most vulnerable to weathering. Iron railings, gates and other decorative work were invariably painted as a protection against rust.

The first colour choice was black, or a russet red, though there is a seventeenth-century drawing by John Smythson of an Inigo Jones house in the Strand, which shows the railing picked out in bright green. Bright green and blue, both being more costly colours, were used for display purposes on metalwork on grander houses, sometimes in conjunction with gold leaf – which is itself an effective protective finish. The blue used for superior work was 'smalt', a vivid colour obtained from crushing a brilliant blue glass to powder. The poor man's version of this admired colour was indigo, usually extended with white lead to make a cheaper 'lead colour'.

Palladian restraint ensured that by the mid-eighteenth century almost all exterior ironwork – which now included balconies – was painted black. Against the stone – or stone-coloured stucco – favoured for later neo-Classical buildings, something richer than black was thought suitable. Sir John Soane specified olive green for one client's house; Royal Blue was used on railings at Somerset House; and Humphrey Repton suggested that a bronze effect, obtained by powdering copper or gold dust over a green ground, was the most handsome finish for cast-iron external detailing. The restrained opulence of a bronzed finish is a good choice against stone and stucco. Where a little more colour is needed, a paint colour imitating the blue-green of weathered copper – verdigris – makes an attractive alternative, popular in major Scandinavian cities.

## THE ULTIMATE FRONT DOOR

There are front doors which are plainly painted, but with a shine so deep and lustrous and a surface so immaculate that they stand out in a street of front doors, like one thoroughbred in a stable of hacks. Dutch cities have more of these immaculate portals per street than anywhere else in Europe, due to the excellence of their paint and the thoroughness of their painters, but the most celebrated individual door in the world must belong to number 10 Downing Street – home to British Prime Ministers – and it is gratifying to see that it too has a truly distinguished gleam.

A paint finish like this is the legitimate descendant of the traditional coach painters'

handiwork. Flawless as a mirror, the secret of achieving it is – simply – elbow grease. It takes many layers of paint, thinly brushed out in the traditional fashion, plus many hours of patient rubbing down of the successive coats with even finer grades of abrasive paper, to achieve a quality finish.

The objectives of the rubbing-down process are as follows: to polish off any grit or dust which might have settled on the drying paint; to level off the surface over all; and to compact the successive paint layers together to create a finish that is bonded to the wood beneath. Some painters use wet-and-dry abrasive paper, lubricated with water, for the rubbing down; others have been known to rub their dry paper over a bar of soap. No one in this league, however, would dream of using an automatic sander – perish the thought! For the final coats (one full strength

*The perhaps not-so-perfect door at Number 10 Downing Street.*

over one thinned with turps or white spirit), a good quality gloss paint, containing plenty of linseed oil, is used. It will not be left glossy as it comes from the can; a final gentle burnishing with powdered pumice or rottenstone, applied with an oily pad of flannel or felt, reduces that vulgar brilliance to the requisite cool smooth aristocratic lustre.

A finish like this lasts for years – decades even. When refurbishment is required, the surface is merely abraded a bit more fiercely than usual and new layers of thin gloss paint, patiently polished as before, go on top. To a certain extent, the perfect front door – like the immaculate lawn – is the result of generations of care and attention.

imposing a classical monumentality on buildings. In keeping with this aspiration, window frames and glazing bars began to be painted in dark colours: black; dark brown and dark blue, so as to create the effect of windows as 'voids' within the architectural scheme. In the better type of house, exterior paintwork was frequently grained in imitation of oak or mahogany. Green paintwork was considered suitable for modest cottage windows and other detail, surrounded as they were by natural greenery.

As the nineteenth century progressed, white increasingly fell out of favour because of its 'staring, glaring colour'. Black, purple, brown and dark green became the preferred exterior colours during the Victorian period.

# DIRECTORY
# OF
# SOURCES

## BRITISH SUPPLIERS

### Architectural Salvage

Architectural Salvage
Netley House
Gomshall, Surrey
GU5 9QA
Tel: 0486 413221
Fax: 0486 412911
*Agency holding large index of architectural component sources; annual registration fee required*

Bridgwater Reclamation Ltd
Monmouth Street
Bridgwater, Somerset
TA6 5EQ
Tel: 0278 424636
*Exterior and interior architectural salvage*

Brighton Architectural Salvage
33 Gloucester Road
Brighton, East Sussex
BN1 4AQ
Tel: 0273 681656
*Exterior and interior period architectural components*

Counterparts Demolition Ltd
Station Yard
Topsham, Exeter
Devon EX3 0EF
Tel: 039 287 5995
*Second-hand doors, slates, tiles, wood, etc*

T. Crowther & Son Ltd
282 North End Road
London SW6 1NH
Tel: 071 385 1375
Fax: 071 386 8353
*Garden ornaments and architectural features, specializing in the Georgian*

H.R. Demolition Ltd
Fairwater Yard
Staplegrove Road

Taunton, Somerset
Tel: 0823 337035
*Second-hand building materials, including roofing tiles, slates, wood, bricks*

Drummonds of Bramley
Birtley Farm, Horsham Road, Bramley
Guildford, Surrey GU5 0LA
Tel: 0483 898766
*Reclaimed building materials, architectural antiques*

The London Architectural Salvage & Supply Company Ltd
Mark Street
(off Paul Street)
London EC2A 4BR
Tel: 071 739 0448/9
Fax: 071 779 6853
*Stone balustrading, old brick and york stone, granite sets, old lighting fixtures*

Woodstock (Totnes) Ltd
Station Road
Totnes, Devon PQ9 5JG
Tel: 0803 864610
Fax: 0803 865401
*Period doors, windows, general architectural components*

### Exterior Paints and Plasters

Artex Ltd
Artex Avenue
Newhaven, East Sussex
BN9 9DD
Tel: 0273 513100
Fax: 0273 515945
*Various textured paints*

BP Aquaseal Ltd
Kingsnorth, Hoo
Rochester, Kent ME3 9ND
Tel: 0634 250722

*Belsize Park, London*

Fax: 0634 253601
*Various wood preservatives*

Crown Berger Europe Ltd
Paints Division
Crown House, Hollins Road
Darwen
Lancashire BB3 0BG
Tel: 0254 704951
Fax: 0254 774414
*Wide range of external paints*

Cuprinol Ltd
Adderwell
Frome, Somerset
BA11 1NL
Tel: 0373 65151
Fax: 0373 74124
*Transparent and tinted wood preservatives*

Imperial Chemical Industries plc

*Clare, Suffolk*

Paints Division
Wexham Road
Slough SL2 5DS
Tel: 0753 31151
Fax: 0753 78218
*Wide range of exterior paints and wood stains*

International Paints plc
Stoneygate Lane, Felling on Tyne, Gateshead
Tyne and Wear NE10 0JY
Tel: 091 469 6111
Fax: 091 438 3711
*Protective external coatings*

Leyland Paint and Wallpaper plc
Paint Division
Huddersfield Road
Birstall, Batley
West Yorkshire WF17 5YN
Tel: 0924 477201
*Preservative wood stains and primers*

Manders Paints Ltd
PO Box 9
Old Heath Road
Heath Town
Wolverhampton
West Midlands WV1 2XG
Tel: 0902 871028
Fax: 0902 52435
*Range of external paints, wall coatings, wood stains and special paints*

Period Mouldings Ltd
11A Westgate Street
Gloucester GL1 2NW
Tel: 0432 352178
Fax: 0432 352112
*Interior and exterior ornamental plasterwork*

The Plaster Decoration Company Ltd
30 Stannary Street
London SE11 4AE
Tel: 071 735 8161
*Plasters, renderings, ornamental fibrous plaster*

Signpost Paints
Haverhill, Suffolk
CB9 8PQ
Tel: 0440 703611
Fax: 0440 706192
*Wood preservatives in natural and various stains*

Snowcem PMC Ltd
Snowcem House
Tharapia Lane
Croydon, Surrey
CR9 4BY
Tel: 081 684 8936
Fax: 081 684 8936 ext 260
*Wide range of cement/sand renders*

### Door and Window Fittings

Architectural Components Ltd
(Locks and Handles)
4–10 Exhibition Road
London SW7 2HF
Tel: 071 581 2401
Fax: 071 509 4928
*Reproduction fittings for doors, windows*

Beardmore Architectural Ironmongery
3 Percy Street
London W1P 0EJ
Tel: 071 637 7041
Fax: 071 436 9222
*Reproduction brass fittings*

Brass Art Craft Birmingham Ltd
76 Atwood Street, Lye
Stourbridge
West Midlands DY9 8RY
Tel: 0384 894814
Fax: 0384 423824
*Period brass window and door fittings*

Hope Works Ltd
Pleck Road, Walsall
West Midlands WS2 9HH
Tel: 0922 720072

Fax: 0922 720080
*Window and door
furniture in brass and iron,
architectural ironmongery*

Perkins & Powell
Cobden Works
Leopold Street
Birmingham B12 0UJ
Tel: 021 772 2303
Fax: 021 772 3334
*Window and door fittings,
ironmongery, hinges,
architectural ironmongery*

## Window Manufacturers and Glaziers

Beverly Bryon
Prisms Stained Glass
    Design
34 Boundary Road
Swiss Cottage
London NW8 0HG
Tel 071 624 5812
*Restoration and new
commissions in stained
glass*

Crittal Windows Ltd
Manor Works, Braintree
Essex CM7 6DF
Tel: 0376 24106
Fax: 0376 49662
*Wide range of
manufactured windows*

Goddard & Gibbs Studio
41–49 Kingsland Road
London E2 8AD
Tel: 071 739 6563
Fax: 071 739 1979
*Stained glass, acid-etched,
sand-blasted glass
windows, panels*

James Hatley & Co Ltd
Beresford Avenue
Wembley, Middlesex
HA0 1RP
Tel: 081 993 2002
Fax: 081 992 6515
*Wide range of antique and
reproduction glass*

Illumin Glass Studio
82 Bond Street
Macclesfield, Cheshire
SK11 6QS
Tel: 0625 613600
*Commissions for stained
glass windows and lights*

Kentel Joinery Ltd
Unit 27, Smiths Industrial
    Estate, Humber Avenue
Coventry, West Midlands
CV3 1JL
Tel: 0203 449621
Fax: 0203 457767
*Manufacturers of
reproduction joinery*

Mumford & Wood Ltd
Joinery Manufacturers
Hallsford Bridge
    Industrial Estate
Ongar, Essex CM5 9RB
Tel: 0277 362401
Fax: 0277 365093
*Manufacturers of
Georgian-, Regency- and
Victorian-style double-
hung sash windows*

Pilkington Glass Ltd
Prescot Road, St Helens
Merseyside WA10 3TT
Tel: 0744 692000
Fax: 0744 692660
*Wide range of glass*

A. H. Pemberton Ltd
63 Shaw Street
Liverpool L6 1HN
Tel: 051 207 1678
Fax: 051 298 1057
*Acid-etched glass, stained
glass, leaded lights made to
order*

SW82 Designs
38A Darwin Road
London W5
Tel: 081 569 8220
*Decorative glass windows,
panels, conservatory
inserts*

## Bricks and Tiling

Baggeridge Brick plc
Gospel End, Sedgley
Dudley, West Midlands
DY3 4AA
Tel: 0902 880555
Fax: 0902 880432
*Wide range of bricks*

Butterley Brick Ltd
Head Office, Wellington
    Street, Ripley, Derby
DE5 3DZ
Tel: 0773 570570
Fax: 0773 570575
*Wide range of bricks,
including specials*

Castlenau Tiles
175 Church Road
Barnes, London SW13
Tel: 081 748 9042
Fax: 081 741 5316
*Terracotta, glazed and
marble tiles*

Ibstock Building
    Products Ltd
Ibstock, Leicester
LE6 1HS
Tel: 0530 60531
Fax: 0530 2584
*Wide range of bricks, tiles,
paving*

The Michelmersh Brick
    Company Ltd
Hillview Road
Michelmersh, Romsey
Hants S051 0NN
Tel: 0794 68506
Fax: 0794 68845
*Wide range of bricks*

Redland Bricks
Graylands, Horsham
Sussex RH12 4QG
Tel: 0403 211222
Fax: 0403 210777
*Manufacturer of wide
range of bricks*

Salvesen Brick Ltd
Adswood Road, Cheadle
    Hulme, Cheadle
Cheshire SK8 5QY
Tel: 061 485 8211
Fax: 061 486 1968
*Traditional stock bricks*

H. & E. Smith Ltd
Van Delft, Britannic
    Works, Broom Street
Nanley, Stoke-on-Trent
Staffordshire ST1 2BR
Tel: 0782 281617
Fax: 0782 269882
*Restoration of old tiles*

## Sources of Information, Skilled Craftsmen

Ancient Monuments
    Society
St Andrew by the
    Wardrobe, Queen
    Victoria Street
London EC4V 5DE
Tel: 071 236 3934
*Conservation of ancient
monuments, old
craftsmanship*

Art Workers Guild
6 Queens Square
London WC1N 3AR
Tel: 071 837 3474
*Guild of craftsmen,
architects and artists,
referral service*

Brick Development
    Association
Woodside House
Winkfield, Windsor
Berkshire SL4 2DX
Tel: 0344 885651
Fax: 0344 890121
*Technical information and
referral service*

British Artist
    Blacksmiths Assoc
c/o Shepley Dawson
Architectural
    Engineering Ltd
Joseph Noble Road
Lilyhall, Workington
Cumbria CA14 4JX
Tel: 0900 68368
Fax: 0900 605911
*Technical information and
referral service*

British Blind and Shutter
    Association
Heath Street, Tamworth
Staffordshire B79 7JH
Tel: 0827 52337
Fax: 0827 310827
*Technical information and
referral service*

British Ceramic Tile
    Council
Federation House
Station Road
Stoke-on-Trent
Staffordshire ST4 2RT
Tel: 0782 747147
Fax: 0782 744102
*Technical information and
referral service*

*Tortola, Virgin Islands*

British Glass
    Manufacturers
    Confederation

Northumberland Road
Sheffield SL0 2UA
Tel: 0742 686201
Fax: 0742 681073
*Technical information and
referral service*

British Wood Preserving
    Association
6 Office Village
4 Romford Road
Stratford, London
E15 4EA
Tel: 081 519 2588
Fax: 081 519 3444
*Technical information and
referral service*

British Woodworking
    Federation
82 New Cavendish Street
London W1M 8AD
Tel: 071 580 5588
Fax: 071 631 3872
*Technical information and
referral service*

The Brooking Collection
C. B. Brooking
Woodhaye, White Lane
Guildford, Surrey
GU4 8PU
Tel: 0483 504555
*Collection of
approximately 20,000
period architectural
building components for
reference; occasional items
for sale*

The Building Centre
26 Store Street
London WC1E 7BT
Tel: 071 637 1022
Fax: 071 580 9641
*Wide range of samples
held, advisory service*

College of Masons
42 Magdalen Road
Wandsworth Common
London SW18 3NP
Tel: 081 874 8363
Fax: 081 871 1342
*Referral service*

Decorative Paving and
    Walling Association
60 Charles Street
Leicester LE1 1FB
Tel: 0533 536161
Fax: 0535 514568
*Information and referral
service*

Door & Shutter
  Manufacturers
  Association
Heath Street, Tamworth
Staffordshire B79 7JH
Tel: 0827 52337
Fax: 0827 310827
*Technical information and
referral service*

Dry Stone Walling
  Association
YFC Centre, National
  Agricultural Centre
Kenilworth
Warwickshire CV8 2LG
Tel: 021 378 0493
*Instructional books and
referral service*

Farm & Rural Building
  Centre
National Agricultural
  Centre, Stoneleigh
Kenilworth
Warwickshire CV8 2LG
Tel: 0203 696503
*Consultancy and enquiry
service*

Federation of Master
  Builders
Gordon Fisher House
14–15 Great James St
London WC1N 3DP
Tel: 071 242 7583
Fax: 071 404 0296
*Information and referral
service*

Fencing Contractors
  Association
St Johns House
23 St Johns Road
Watford, Hertfordshire
WD1 1PY
Tel: 0923 248895
Fax: 0923 31134
*Referral service*

*Charleston, S. Carolina*

The Georgian Group
37 Spital Square
London E1 6DY
Tel: 071 377 1722
Fax: 071 247 3441
*Advises on preservation
and repair of Georgian
buildings*

Glass and Glazing
  Federation
44 Borough High Street
London SE1 1XB
Tel: 071 403 7177
*Technical information*

Guild of Architectural
  Ironmongers
8 Stepney Green
London E1 3JU
Tel: 071 790 3431
Fax: 071 790 8517
*Technical information and
referral service*

The Guild of Master
  Craftsmen
166 High Street, Lewes
East Sussex BN7 1YE
Tel: 0273 477374
Fax: 0273 478606
*Publishes* Guide to
Restoration Experts,
*referral service*

London Association of
  Master Stonemasons
82 New Cavendish Street
London W1M 8AD
Tel: 071 580 5588
Fax: 071 631 3872
*Referral service*

London Master Plasterers
  Association
82 New Cavendish Street
London W1M 8AD
Tel: 071 580 5588
Fax: 071 631 3872
*Referral service*

Men of the Stones
The Rutland Studio
Tinwell, Stamford
Lincolnshire PE9 3UD
Tel: 0780 63372
*Conservation of stone
buildings, technical
information and referral
service*

National Society of
  Master Thatchers
High View, Little Street

*San Diego, California*

Yardley, Hastings
Northamptonshire
*Consultancy and referral
service*

Paintmakers Association
  of Great Britain
Alembic House
93 Albert Embankment
London SE1 7TY
Tel: 071 582 1185
Fax: 071 735 0616
*Information and referral
service*

Thatching Advisory
  Service Ltd
Rose Tree Farm
29 Nine Mile Ride
Finchampstead
Wokingham, Berkshire
RS11 4QD
Tel: 0734 734203
Fax: 0734 328054
*Information, surveys and
referral service*

The Thirties Society
18 Comeragh Road
London W14 9HP
Tel: 071 382 9797
*Technical information,
publications on preserving
buildings of 1914–1960*

Timber Trade Federation
Clareville House
26–27 Oxenden Street
London SW1Y 4EL
Tel: 071 839 1891
Fax: 071 930 0094
*Technical information*

The Victorian Society
1 Priory Gardens
London W4 1TT
Tel: 081 994 1019
*Advises on protection and
repairs of Victorian and
Edwardian buildings*

## Decorative Ironwork

Artistic Ironworkers
  Supplies Ltd
Wrought Iron Works
Unit 1, Whitehouse
  Road, Kidderminster
Worcestershire
DY10 1HT
Tel: 0562 753483
Fax: 0562 820380
*Suppliers of metal
components ready for
fabrication, and index of
skilled metal craftsmen*

Kentish Ironcraft
Ashford Road
Bethersden, Ashford
Kent TN26 3AT
Tel: 023 382 465
Fax: 023 382 805
*Restoration and
reproduction of wrought
iron gates*

Wing & Staples
The Forge, Motcombe
Shaftesbury, Dorset
SP7 9PE
Tel: 0747 53104
*Period reproduction
ironwork undertaken*

*Martha's Vineyard,
Massachusetts*

## Fences and Gates

English Basket Centre
The Willows, Curload
Stoke St Gregory
nr Taunton, Somerset
TA3 6JD
Tel: 0823 69418
*Willow hurdle fencing,
garden screens and arches*

Larch Lap, Ltd
PO Box 17, Lichfield St
Stourport-on-Severn
Worcestershire DY1 3S
Tel: 02993 3232
Fax: 02993 71534
*Larch-lap panels, picket
fences, trellis work*

R. G. Trade Supplies and
  Engineering Ltd
Taurus Ornamental
  Design
Foley Street, Fenton
Stoke-on-Trent, Staffs
ST4 3DR
Tel: 0782 599 125
Fax: 0782 335 367
*Ornamental railings and
gates*

Victorian Lace
Unit 3,
Radford Industrial Estate
Ford, nr Arundel
West Sussex BN18 0BE
Tel: 0903 731030
Fax: 0903 731031
*Fencing, gates and barriers,
architectural ironmongery*

Wyevale Landscapes Ltd
Buckover
Wooton-under-Edge
Gloucester GL12 8QL
Tel: 0454 419175
Fax: 0454 412901
*Wide range of timber and
wire fencing*

## Awnings and Canopies

Abacus Blinds
Old Fire Station
Wheeler Lane, Witley
Godalming, Surrey
GU8 5QU
Tel: 042 879 4757
*Canvas and acylic
conservatory and external
blinds*

American Shutters
72 Station Road
London SW13 0LS
Tel: 081 876 5905
Fax: 081 878 9548
*Window awnings, shutters
and louvres*

The Blind Corner
66a Ferme Park Road
Hornsey, London N4 4ED
Tel: 081 348 4867
Fax: 081 348 6891
*Supplier of custom-made
and standard awnings and
blinds*

E. Boraster & Sons
59 Tower Hamlets Road
Walthamstow

London E17
Tel: 081 520 4288
*Custom-made awnings,
shutters and louvres*

Ericson Blinds Ltd
Canal Wharf, Langley
Slough SL3 6EN
Tel: 0753 580580
Fax: 0753 40880
*Custom-made awnings,
shutters and louvres*

The House of Shutters
200 Westbourne Grove
London W11 2RH
Tel: 071 229 9095
Fax: 071 229 4929
*Custom-made awnings,
shutters and louvres*

## Conservatories

Alexander Bartholomew
277 Putney Bridge Road
London SW17 2PT
Tel: 071 785 7263
Fax: 071 785 9563
*Customized modular and
one-off conservatories*

Amdega Ltd
Faverdale, Darlington
County Durham
DL3 0PW
Tel: 0325 468 522
Fax: 0325 489 209
*Customized modular
conservatories*

Cotswold Buildings Ltd
Standlake, Oxfordshire
OX8 7QG
Tel: 0865 300711
Fax: 0865 300284
*Modular and purpose-built
conservatories*

Finch Conservatories Ltd
2–4 Parham Drive
Boyatt Wood
Eastleigh, Hampshire
SO5 4NU
Tel: 0800 378 168
Fax: 0703 620 195
*Purpose-built
conservatories*

Frost Conservatories Ltd
The Old Forge
Tempsford, Sandy
Bedfordshire SG19 2AG
Tel: 0767 40808
Fax: 0767 40561
*Timber conservatories*

Halls Traditional
  Conservatories
Church Road
Paddock Wood
Tonbridge
Kent TN12 6EU
Tel: 089283 4444
Fax: 089283 3936
*Cedar conservatories*

Machin Designs Ltd
Ransomes Dock
35–37 Parkgate Road
London SW11
Tel: 071 350 1581
Fax: 071 924 2438
*Customized modular
conservatories*

*Baltimore, Maryland*

Marsten & Langinger Ltd
Hall Staithe, Fakenham
Norfolk NR21 9BW
Tel: 0328 864933
Fax: 0328 851067
*Standard designs and
customized conservatories*

Room Outside Ltd
Goodwood Gardens
Goodwood, West
  Sussex PO18 0QB
Tel: 0243 776563
Fax: 0243 776313
*Customized modular
conservatories*

Vale Garden Houses
Melton Road, Harlaxton
Grantham
Lincolnshire NG32 1HQ
Tel: 0476 64433
Fax: 0476 78555
*Customized modular
conservatories and
summerhouses*

Walton Conservatories Ltd
96 Thorpe Lea Road
Egham, Surrey
TW20 8DF
Tel: 0784 461900
Fax: 0784 451829
*Customized timber
conservatories*

## Garden Ornaments and Statuary

Architectural Heritage Ltd
Taddington Manor
Cutsdean
Cheltenham
Gloucestershire
GL54 5RY
Tel: 0386 73414
Fax: 0386 73236
*Antique garden statuary*

Brookbrae Ltd
53 St Leonards Road
London SW14 7NQ
Tel: 081 876 4370
Fax: 081 878 9415
*Sundials in bronze or slate,
cast stone plinths*

The Chelsea Gardener
125 Sydney Street
London SW3 6NR
Tel: 071 352 5656
Fax: 071 352 3301
*Garden ornaments, seats,
trellis*

Chilstone Garden
  Ornaments
Sprivers Estate
Horsmonden, Kent
TN12 8DB
Tel: 089 272 3553
Fax: 089 272 3223
*Reconstituted stone garden
ornaments*

Christie's, South
  Kensington
85 Old Brompton Road
London SW7 3LD
Tel: 071 581 7611
Fax: 071 584 0431
*Auction house with
occasional sales of garden
ornaments and
architectural fittings*

Clifton Nurseries Ltd
Clifton Villas
Warwick Avenue
London W9 2PH
Tel: 071 289 6851
Fax: 071 286 4215
*Antique and contemporary
garden ornaments and
furniture*

Crowther of Syon Lodge
Busch Corner
London Road

Isleworth
Middlesex TW7 5BH
Tel: 081 560 7978
Fax: 081 568 7572
*Antique garden ornaments,
seats, ironwork, etc*

Haddonstone Ltd
The Forge House
East Haddon
Northants NN6 8DB
Tel: 0604 770711
Fax: 0604 770027
*Architectural garden
ornament in reconstructed
stone*

Knight Terrace Pots
West Orchard
Shaftesbury, Dorset
SP7 0LJ
Tel: 0258 72685
*Cast stone garden urns and
sundials*

Minsterstone Ltd
Station Road, Ilminster
Somerset TA19 9A
Tel: 04605 2277
Fax: 04605 7865
*Reconstructed stone
ornaments*

The Olive Tree Trading
  Company Ltd
Twickenham Trading
  Estate, Rugby Road
Twickenham, Middx
TW1 1DG
Tel: 081 892 8031
Fax: 081 744 1527
*Frost-proof terracotta
ornament and seats*

*Washington D.C.*

Renaissance Bronzes Ltd
79 Pimlico Road
London SW1W 8PH
Tel: 071 823 5149
Fax: 071 352 2604
*Bronze statuary*

Renaissance Casting
19 Cranford Road
Coventry CV5 8JF
Tel: 0203 227275
*Lead statuary and garden
ornament*

Robin Eden
Pickwick End, Corsham
Wiltshire SN13 0JB
Tel: 0249 7133353
*Painted wirework gazebos*

Seago Ltd
22 Pimlico Road
London SW1W 8LJ
Tel: 071 730 7502
Fax: 071 730 9179
*Period garden statuary and
ornament*

Shedlow, Harrison
  Joinery Ltd
Stratford Garage
Stratford St Andrew
Saxmundham, Suffolk
IP17 1LF
Tel: 0728 604264
Fax: 0728 603162
*Edwardian-style cast-iron
garden urns, ornaments
and furniture*

Sotheby's
Summers Place
nr Billingshurst, West
  Sussex RH14 9AD
Tel: 0403 783933
Fax: 0403 785153
*Auctions of garden
statuary and architectural
items*

Stuart Garden
  Architecture
Larchfield Estate
Dowlish Ford
Ilminster, Somerset
TA19 0PF
Tel: 0460 57862
Fax: 0460 53525
*Treillage, trelliswork, seats,
arbours, pergolas, gazebos*

## Exterior Lighting

Crompton Parkinson Ltd
Woodland House
The Avenue, Cliftonville
Northants NN1 5BS
Tel: 0604 30201
Fax: 0604 26982
*Spotlights, lighting
bollards, wall lights, etc*

Chilstone Garden
    Ornaments
Sprivors Estate
Horsmonden, Kent
TN12 8DB
Tel: 089 272 3553
Fax: 089 272 3223
*Edwardian reproduction
copper lamps*

Christopher Wray's
    Lighting Emporium
600 King's Road
London SW6 2DX
Tel: 071 736 8434
*Period lighting specialists*

Classic Reproductions Ltd
Unit 16, Highams Lodge
    Business Centre
Blackhorse Lane
London E17 6SH
Tel: 081 531 8627
Fax: 081 531 6056
*Wide range of traditional
lanterns*

Crompton Parkinson Ltd
Woodland House
The Avenue, Cliftonville
Northants NN1 5BS
Tel: 0604 30201
Fax: 0604 26982
*Simple modern lighting
fixtures*

Forma Lighting Ltd
Unit 310, Business
    Design Centre
52 Upper Street
London N1 0QH
Tel: 071 288 6025
Fax: 071 288 6057
*Simple contemporary
Italian fixtures*

Hoffmeister Lighting
Unit 4, Preston Road
Reading, Berkshire
RG2 0BB
Tel: 0734 866941
Fax: 0734 310035
*External and internal
lighting fixtures*

*Old Bennington,
Vermont*

David Hunt Lighting
Tilemans Lane
Shipton-on-Stour
Warwickshire
CV36 4HP
Tel: 0608 61590
Fax: 0608 62951
*Conversion and
restoration of period
lighting, one-off
commissions*

Lighting Design
1 Woodfall Court
Smith Street

London SW3 4EJ
Tel: 071 730 8585
Fax: 071 385 0042
*Interior and exterior
lighting design and fixtures*

Mr Light
275 Fulham Road
London SW10 9PZ
Tel: 071 352 7525
Fax: 071 581 3499
*Wide range of free-
standing and wall-hung
lanterns*

Minsterstone Ltd
Station Road, Ilminster
Somerset
Tel: 04605 2277
Fax: 04605 7865
*Oriental lanterns in
reconstructed stone*

Renzland Ltd,
London Road, Copford
Colchester, Essex
CO6 1LG
Tel: 0206 210212

Fax: 0206 211290
*Wrought-iron lanterns*

Smithbrook Ltd
Smithbrook, Cranleigh
Surrey GU6 8LH
Tel: 0483 272744
Fax: 0483 267863
*Wrought-iron light fittings*

Sugg Lighting Ltd
65 Gatwick Road
Crawley, Sussex
RH10 2YU
Tel: 0293 540111
Fax: 0293 540114
*Traditional Victorian- and
Edwardian-style gas and
electric lighting*

D. W. Windsor Ltd
Pindar Road, Hoddesdon
Hertfordshire
EN11 0EZ
Tel: 0992 445666
Fax: 0992 440493
*Period pedestal and wall-
hung metal lighting*

## AMERICAN SUPPLIERS

### Architectural Salvage

The Bank
1824 Felicity Street
New Orleans, LA 70113
Tel: 504 523 2702
Fax: 504 523 6055
*Doors, shutters, molding,
brackets, gingerbread,
spindles, columns, gates*

Gargoyles Ltd
512 South Third Street
Philadelphia, PA 19147
Tel: 215 629 1700
*Wide variety of exterior
and interior details*

Great American Salvage
    Company
3 Main Street
Montpelier, VT 05602
Tel: 802 223 7711
*Complete selection of
exterior details, including
doors, cresting, columns,
porches, exterior lighting*

Irreplaceable Artifacts
14 Second Avenue,
New York, NY 10003

Tel: 212 777 2900
Fax: 212 777 4112
*Whole façades and parts
thereof in terracotta,
limestone, cast-iron and
bronze*

United House Wrecking
    Corp.
535 Hope Street
Stamford, CT 06920
Tel: 203 348 5371

Urban Archaeology
285 Lafayette Street
New York, NY 10012
Tel: 212 431 6969
Fax: 212 941 1989
*Large selection of exterior
and interior architectural
embellishments*

### Exterior Paints

Benjamin Moore & Co.
51 Chestnut Ridge Road
Montvale, NJ 07645
Tel: 201 573 9600
Fax: 201 573 9046
*Documented historical
colors suitable for
eighteenth- and*

*New Orleans, Louisiana*

*nineteenth-century
exteriors*

Finnaren & Haley
2320 Haverford Road,
Ardmore, PA 19003
Tel: 215 649 5000
*Variety of exterior paints,
including a line of
Victorian colors*

The Glidden Company
925 Euclid Avenue
Cleveland, OH 44115
Tel: 216 344 8000
Fax: 216 344 8900
*Full line of exterior paints,
including historically*

*appropriate colors*

Partridge Replications
83 Grove Street
Peterborough
NH 03458
Tel: 603 924 3002
*24 colors of low-sheen oil-
based paints*

The Sherwin Williams
    Company
101 Prospect Avenue
    N.W.
Cleveland, OH 44115
Tel: 216 566 2000
Fax: 216 566 3310
*Extensive selection of
exterior hues, including
Heritage II line, designed to
reflect a historical look*

Stulb/Allentown Paint
    Manufacturing
    Company
P.O. Box 597
Allentown, PA 18105
Tel: 215 433 4273
Fax: 215 433 6116
*Hold exclusive rights to
historic Old Village and
Sturbridge paints*

### Door and Window Hardware

Arden Forge
301 Brintons Bridge
    Road
West Chester
PA 19382
*Ornamental hardware for
Victorian and Colonial
houses, original and
custom work*

Baldwin Hardware
    Corporation
841 East Wyomissing
    Boulevard
Reading, PA 19612
Tel: 215 777 7811
Fax: 215 777 7256
*Full line of brass hardware
and fittings*

Ball and Ball
463 West Lincoln
    Highway
Exton, PA 19341
Tel: 215 363 7330
Fax: 215 363 7639
*Reproductions of
eighteenth-century
hardware in brass and iron*

Cirecast
380 7th Street
San Francisco, CA 94103
Tel: 415 863 8319
Fax: 415 863 7721
*Historic builder's hardware
of all kinds*

Kayne & Son Custom
 Forged Hardware
76 Daniel Ridge Road
Candler, NC 28715
Tel: 704 667 8868
*Iron and brass hardware,
including custom work*

The Smithy
Wolcott, VT 05680
Tel: 802 472 6508
*All custom work, including
door latches and hinges*

## Glaziers

Blenko Glass Co.
Fairground Road
Milton, WV 25541
Tel: 304 743 9081
Fax: 304 743 0547
*Hand-blown antique-style
glass, including stained
glass, slab glass, and bull's-
eye glass; some custom
work*

Golden Age Glassworks
339 Bellvale Road
Warwick, NY 10990
Tel: 914 986 1487
*All types of Victorian glass,
including windows and
door panels*

Kraatz Russell Glass
Grist Mill Hill
RFD 1, Box 320-C
Canaan, NH 03741
Tel: 603 523 4289
*Contemporary and
historical glass, including
bull's-eye windows and
leaded glass; custom work*

J & R Lamb Studios, Inc.
P.O. Box 291
Philmont, NY 12565
Tel: 518 672 7267
*Create and repair stained
glass*

Andreas Lehmann/
 Thomas Tisch
1793 12th Street
Oakland, CA 94607

Tel: 415 465 7158
*Creation and restoration of
fine custom glass,
including decorative
windows, Victorian cut
glass*

Rambusch
40 West 13th Street
New York, NY 10011
Tel: 212 675 0400
Fax: 212 620 4687
*Creation and restoration of
arts and crafts glass*

Morgan Bockius Studios
 Inc.
1412 York Road
Warminster, PA 18974
Tel: 215 672 6547
*Custom leaded, beveled,
and carved glass and
restoration*

*Washington D.C.*

## Bricks and Tiling

Boren Clay Products
P.O. Box 368
Pleasant Garden
NC 27313
Tel: 919 674 2255
Fax: 919 674 5397
*Manufacture and sell
many varieties of brick*

Continental Clay
 Company
260 Oak Avenue
Kittanning, PA 16201
Tel: 412 543 2611
Fax: 412 545 9659
*Specialize in red, buff, and
gray building brick*

Dunis Studios
HC 53, Box 3125
Bulverde, Texas 78163
Tel: 512 438 7715
*Hand-painted ceramic tile
for pools, fountains,
external murals*

Gladding McBean
P.O. Box 97
Lincoln, CA 95648
Tel: 916 645 3341
Fax: 916 645 1723
*Manufacturers of
terracotta architectural
and roofing tile since 1875*

Glen-Gery Corporatioin
1166 Spring Street
Wyomissing, PA 19610
Tel: 215 374 4011
Fax: 215 374 1622
*Manufacturers of extruded,
molded, and handmade
brick*

Richard Thomas Keit
 Studios
1396 Sheffield Place
Thousand Oaks
CA 91360
Tel: 805 495 5032
*Fine reproductions of
historic Malibu patio tiles*

Rising & Nelson Slate
 Co., Inc.
Box 98
West Pawlett, VT 05775
Tel: 802 645 0150
*Manufacturers and
suppliers of roofing slate in
a variety of colors*

Smith & Hawken
25 Corte Madera
Mill Valley, CA 94941
Tel: 415 383 2000
*Reproduction Victorian
edging tiles*

*Charleston, S. Carolina*

Starbuck Goldner Studio
315 West Fourth Street
Bethlehem, PA 18015
Tel: 215 866 6321
*Designers and
manufacturers of*

*handmade tile; will match
and reproduce antique
tiles*

## Exterior Decoration Specialists

Architectural
 Reclamation, Inc.
312 South River Street
Franklin, OH 45005
Tel: 513 746 8964
*General exterior
contracting, with a
specialty in historic
structures and log
buildings*

*Columbus, Ohio*

Arlan Kay & Associates
110 King Street
Madison, WI 53703
Tel: 608 251 7515
*Full-service architectural
firm with expertise in
rehabilitation and
recycling*

David M. LaPenta
215 Sheeder Road
Phoenixville, PA 19460
Tel: 215 627 2782
*Architectural and general
contracting services for all
structures*

Oehrlein & Associates
1702 Connecticut
 Avenue, N.W.
Washington, D.C. 20009
Tel: 202 387 8040
*Preservation architects
providing full
architectural services on
all aspects of historical
and non-historical
structures*

Restorations Unlimited
 Inc.

24 West Main Street
Elizabethville, PA 17023
Tel: 717 362 3477
*General contractors
specializing in all facets of
older houses; will
manufacture any type of
specialty millwork*

Skyline Engineers of
 Maryland, Inc.
5405 Beall Drive
Frederick, MD 21701
Tel: 301 831 8800
*Restoration and
preservation specialists,
doing custom carpentry,
masonry, lighting,
painting, ornamental
copperwork, gilding*

Townsend Anderson
RD1, Box 860
Moretown, VT 05660
Tel: 802 244 5095
*Specialists in exterior
renovation and
restoration, solving
structural problems,
recreative exterior
decoration*

## Garden Ornament and Statuary

Cape Cod Cupola
78 State Road
North Dartmouth
MA 02747
Tel: 508 994 2119
*Cupolas, birthbaths,
weathervanes, sundials,
lanterns*

Florentine Craftsmen
46–24 28th Street
Long Island City
NY 11101
Tel: 718 937 7632
Fax: 718 937 9858
*Handcrafted lead garden
ornaments; fountains of
lead, aluminium and
stone; custom work*

Fountains of Wayne
491 Route 46
Wayne, NJ 07470
Tel: 201 256 1552
Fax: 201 256 1348
*Fountains, cast-concrete
garden statuary and
planters*

Gardener's Eden
P.O. Box 7307
San Francisco, CA 94120
Tel: 415 421 4242
*Planters, statuary, wall plaques, garden arches, birdbaths*

*Annapolis, Maryland*

International Terra Cotta Inc.
690 North Robertson Boulevard
Los Angeles, CA 90069
Tel: 213 657 3752
*Terracotta urns, statuary, planters, wall plaques; branches in Atlanta, GA, and Dania, Fl*

Nostalgia
307 Stiles Avenue
Savannah, GA 31401
Tel: 912 232 2324
Fax: 912 234 5746
*Fountains, wrought-iron benches, weathervanes, statuary*

Robinson Iron Corporation
P.O. Box 1119
Robinson Road
Alexander City
AL 35010
Tel: 205 329 8486
Fax: 205 329 8960
*Iron and aluminium fountains, urns and furniture*

Sculpture Cast
P.O. Box 426
Roosevelt, NJ 08555
Tel: 609 426 0942
*Limited-edition original*

*pieces of garden sculpture in cast stone and bronze*

Sculpture Design Imports, Inc.
416 South Robertson Boulevard
Los Angeles, CA 90048
Tel: 213 858 8266
*Fountains, statuary, terracotta urns*

Smith & Hawken
25 Corte Madera
Mill Valley, CA 94941
Tel: 415 383 2000
*Planters in teak, terracotta, and fiberglass*

Winterthur Museum and Gardens
Winterthur, DE 19735
Tel: 800 767 0500
*Birdbaths, planters, garden sculpture*

## Outdoor Lighting

A.J.P. Coppersmith & Co.
20 Industrial Parkway
Woburn, MA 01801
Tel: 617 245 1216
Fax: 617 932 3704
*Handcrafted reproduction Colonial outdoor lighting, including post lights and wall lanterns in copper and brass*

Hanover Lantern
470 High Street
Hanover, PA 17331
Tel: 717 632 6464
Fax: 717 632 5039
*Wide variety of outdoor lighting fixtures*

Loran, Inc.
1705 East Colton Avenue
Redlands, CA 92373
Tel: 714 794 2121
*Outdoor lighting fixtures*

Spring City Electrical Manufacturing Company
Hall and Main Streets, Drawer A
Spring City, PA 19475
Tel: 215 948 4000
Fax: 215 948 5577
*Ornamental lamp posts, light boxes*

Wendelighting
9068 Culver Boulevard
Culver City, CA 90230
Tel: 213 559 4310
*Variety of landscape lighting fixtures*

## Roofers and Masons

Geary Roofing Service
1330 Lawrence Street
El Cerrito, CA 94530
Tel: 415 237 7088
*Cedar shingle and tile roofing, specializing in renovations and restorations*

Harne Plastering Company
P.O. Box 22
Libertytown, MD 21762
Tel: 301 898 5606
*Masonry repair, specializing in plaster and stucco restoration*

Jeff Alte Roofing
P.O. Box 639
Somerville, NJ 08876
Tel: 201 526 2111
*Restoration specialist*

Skyline Engineers of Maryland, Inc.
5405 Beall Drive
Frederick, MD 21701
Tel: 301 831 8800
*Masonry repair and preservation*

## Decorative Ironwork

G. Krug & Son, Inc.
415 West Saratoga Street
Baltimore, MD 21201
Tel: 301 752 3166
*All kinds of decorative ironwork, including gates, balconies, fences, railings; custom work, including bootscrapers, shutter holdbacks*

Kenneth Lynch & Sons, Inc.
84 Danbury Road
P.O. Box 488
Wilton, CT 06897
Tel: 203 762 8363
Fax: 203 762 2999
*Wide variety of*

*ornamental ironwork including iron gates*

New England Tool Company
P.O. Box 30
Chester, NY 10918
Tel: 914 782 5332
*Architectural metalwork, including grillwork, window guards and railings*

Tennessee Fabricating Co.
1822 Latham Street
Memphis, TN 38106
Tel: 901 948 3354
Fax: 901 948 3356
*Custom casting work, including ornamental metal, cast iron, and cast aluminium*

## Fences, Walls, and Gates

Mad River Woodworks
189 Taylor Way
P.O. Box 1067
Blue Lake, CA 95525
Tel: 707 668 5671
*Complete line of Victorian-era gingerbread, all wood*

New England Tool Company
P.O. Box 30
Chester, NY 10918
Tel: 914 782 5332
*Estate fencing in ornamental iron, electronically controlled driveway gates*

Stewart Ironworks Co.
P.O. Box 2612
Covington, KY 41012
Tel: 606 431 1985
Fax: 606 431 2035
*Custom ornamental iron fencing and gates, specializing in Victorian styles*

## Porches and Conservatories

Amdega Conservatories Inc.
Boston Design Centre
Suite 624
660 Summer Street
Boston, MA 02210

Tel: 800 922 0110
Fax: 617 951 2717
*Handcrafted conservatories made in England since 1874*

Gazebo and Porchworks
728 9th Avenue, S.W.
Puyallup, WA 98371
Tel: 206 848 0502
*Manufacture complete line of elements for wood porches and gazebos, including corbels, corner brackets, porch swings, spindles, railings*

Gothic Arch Greenhouses
P.O. Box 1564
Mobile, AL 36633
Tel: 800 628 4974
*Prefabricated greenhouses of redwood and fiberglass*

*Door in Vermont*

Janco
9390 Davis Avenue
Laurel, MD 20207
Tel: 800 323 6933
*Solariums, greenhouses, and accessories*

Lord & Burnham
Irvington
NY 10533
Tel: 914 591 8800
*Modern conservatories*

Machin Designs (USA)
652 Glenbrook Road
Stamford, CT 06907
Tel: 203 834 9566
*Customized modular conservatories*

# GLOSSARY

**Aggregate**
Mineral particles of various types and sizes mixed with cement or plaster to make concrete.

**Coarse aggregate** is made using small particles no smaller than 3/16in/4.5mm and produces a very rough finish.

**Fine aggregate** is usually made with sand, for plaster and final rendering where a smooth finish is required.

**Heavy aggregate** uses crushed bricks and stone and is usually for rough-cast concrete.

**Light aggregate** uses coke breeze, pumice or foamed slag from furnaces and makes inexpensive building blocks.

**Architraves**
The main beam resting on two or more columns. More commonly, the masonry frame around a door, window or arch or the timber mouldings which cover the joints between door and window casings and the plaster of the walls.

**Ashlar**
Masonry of hewn stones, usually in thin slabs to form a facing for a building.

**Barge-board (verge- or gable-board)**
Pieces of timber which cover the ends of roof timbers on the gable ends of buildings. They are often ornamentally carved or highly decorated.

**Breezeblock (cinderblock)**
Flat slabs of compressed cinder-dust, made from the manufacture of bricks, commonly used as an inexpensive lining for the interiors of buildings.

**Cement**
Mixture of chalk, limestone, clay and a little gypsum with water which is used to bond bricks or stones or is the binding medium in an aggregate.

**Cills (sills)**
The lower horizontal part of a door or window frame.

**Concrete**
Mixture of cement, sand, water and aggregate so balanced as to ensure a very hard set.

**Bush-hammered concrete** has had its surface roughened to expose the particles of aggregate.

**Pre-stressed concrete** is laid around a framework of steel cables under tension. This tension is released once the concrete has set hard and this has the effect of compressing the concrete and increasing its tensile strength.

**Reinforced concrete** sets around steel rods or mesh.

**Corbel**
Block of stone, often decoratively carved, projecting from a wall as a support.

**Course**
One complete horizontal row of bricks or stones.

**Distemper**
A method of painting walls in which the pigments are mixed with size dissolved in water; usually applied to a ground of chalk or plaster mixed with gum.

**Dovecot**
Small house for birds which is either freestanding as an out-house or is built on to a house as a sort of balcony, roof extension or air vent. They are often elaborate and highly decorated.

**Dressing**
Any form of projecting moulding other than plain surfaces, eg ashlar facing, cills, quoins etc.

**Fenestration**
The arrangement, relationship and appearance of windows on a building.

**Furrow**
A channel or groove: to make channels or grooves.

**Hammer-dress**
To give the surface of stone a rough finish, usually for rustication and particularly associated with sandstone.

**Header**
A brick or stone with its head or end in the face of a wall.

**Limewash**
A mixture of lime and water used to coat walls in order to preserve and decorate.

**Mortar**
Mixture of lime or cement with sand and water which is used to join, bed and point bricks or stone.

**Oriel window**
A bay window on an upper floor, or projecting from the face of a wall on the ground floor, usually supported by brackets or corbelling.

**Pebble dash**
Exterior surface of stucco or plaster on which small pebbles have been applied before the render has set completely.

**Pointing**
A finishing for the joints of brickwork or masonry using a mortar which is thicker than that used for bedding the bricks or stones. It is often coloured to blend or contrast.

**Flush pointing** has the mortar laid on thickly enough to fill the joints completely and then smoothed flush to produce a continuous surface.

**Struck** or **weathered pointing** is done in a way to ensure that the mortar slopes downwards to throw off rain water.

**Bucket-handle pointing** produces rounded indentations.

**Square-recessed pointing** is deep set to produce square-edged grooves.

**Portico**
Structure of columns, usually around a door.

**Quoin**
One of the bricks or stones forming an external angle of a wall or building.

**Rendering**
Surface covering of a wall, composed of mortar or plaster. In interior plasterwork the term is usually used of the first coat of plaster; in exteriors it is normally the final coating, often of cement and sand.

**Reveal**
A side of an opening or recess which is at right angles to the face of the surface, especially used of the vertical sides of a door or window opening between the frame and the wall.

**Rough-cast**
Coarse-textured exterior surface obtained by mixing gravel or shingle with the final coat of rendering.